MW00629461

The
Mythopoetic
Impulse

The

Mythopoetic
Impulse

SELECTED ESSAYS 2017-2022

BRADLEY OLSON

JOSEPH CAMPBELL
FOUNDATION

Copyright © 2023 Joseph Campbell Foundation All rights reserved. No part of this publication may be reproduced, distributed, or transmitted in any form or by any means, including photocopying, recording, or other electronic or mechanical methods, without the prior written permission of the publisher, except in the case of brief quotations embodied in critical reviews and certain other noncommercial uses permitted by copyright law. For permission requests, please contact the Joseph Campbell Foundation's Rights and Permissions Manager at rights@jcf.org.

Paperback ISBN: 978-1-61178-037-6
Ebook ISBN: 978-1-61178-042-0

Front cover image detail from The School of Athens by Raphael

Book design by *the*BookDesigners

First printing edition 2023

www.jcf.org

For Roxanne and Lilia, and for Robert Walter.
And of course, for Joseph Campbell, who urged us
to make the great leap into our own inward mystery.

Contents

Author's Introduction

The essays contained in this book were previously published on the Joseph Campbell Foundation website (jcf.org) and in JCF's MythBlast, a weekly newsletter that contains an essay interpreting a monthly theme within the context of a highlighted work by Joseph Campbell. We intend for MythBlasts to deliver little "blasts" of mythology that would introduce readers to a deeper, more considered understanding of myth and Joseph Campbell's work.

We began publishing essays in 2017. I and Dr. Leigh Melander, who was at the time vice president of the JCF Board, wrote all the MythBlasts, and in the beginning they were quite short, a paragraph of about three hundred to four hundred words or so, which related mythological topics or events tied to the year's calendar. There is hardly a day of the year that doesn't have some sort of mythological connection. Some, like Christmas, Rosh Hashanah, Ramadan, are well known events, but we also focused attention on other, perhaps less well-known yet regularly celebrated, myth-related calendar dates. MythBlasts were immediately popular with readers who received the newsletter or followed the latest activities and publications of the Joseph Campbell Foundation.

Because of that popularity, the length and focus of MythBlasts evolved into longer, more thoughtful essays on Campbell, mythology, and even occasional forays into theories of myth. The MythBlast series has grown to become one of the central features of the Joseph Campbell Foundation website and its internet presence. Presently, the MythBlast series has published hundreds of original essays that have highlighted and explored various Campbell texts, and they continue to be written in an accessible yet intelligent manner that has challenged our readers to be thoughtful and, at the same time, whetted appetites for reading more widely in Campbell's works.

Rather than focus on what I think the images of myth mean in my contributions to the MythBlast series, my goal was to focus on what myth does to us, how *it* understands *us*; how the images of myth and its various narratives work in the imaginations of those billions of people who comprise our collective consciousness. I wanted to convey how mythic narratives empower us, how they connect us to unconscious vulnerabilities, how they can console and encourage us, and how they place us in a more harmonious relationship to the conditions of life, conditions that long predate human life on this planet and are not always congenial to the human animal.

By rooting the exploration of mythology in imagination rather than in cultural or religious or even psychological traditions, the narratives are freed from historical, literary, and orthodox contexts. Myth is then free to live as an imaginal exploration, as a meditation on the images and narratives of myth, which allows one to explore and question how high-value, symbolic images organize and determine our lives and, of course, the cultures in which we do the living. Those questions ultimately lead one to asking the big question: Is the way I live my life aligned with my true passions? Does it allow me to live compassionately, courageously, and honestly in my daily life?

Compassion, courage, and honesty are some of the foundational elements of bliss, and they serve as a kind of gyroscope that, if we build a life around them, will unleash the potential for living into the unique possibilities we have available to express in the world. Living such a life is the verse we may, to gloss Walt Whitman, contribute to the powerful play that is not merely our own lives but the lives of the collective, and the life of the world itself.

Using myth in this way—thinking mythically, one might say—opens the doors of perception to astonishment and delight, to curiosity, to life's festival of passing forms, of life with its full range of emotion and experience. It liberates the sublime embedded in human experience with all its passions and sufferings, changes of fortune, joys, depressions—its pathos as well as its ecstasy. While thinking mythically won't allow us to remake the world, it does allow us to remake ourselves.

The essays selected for this volume have all been published in previous MythBlast newsletters and on the Joseph Campbell Foundation MythBlast website. I have edited some of these essays for clarity and errors in grammar and punctuation. The first section of essays consists of MythBlasts that were written earlier in the life of the series and connect to celebrations determined by the particular day or time of year. The second section deals more with the mythopoetics of the literature of myth, and touches on its relationship to psychology, literature, and philosophy as they pertain to mythopoesis, the making of myths, and mythography. The last section offers an exploration of heroism and the hero.

I always ended each MythBlast I wrote with four words, and I say them now to you, the reader, with the utmost gratitude and appreciation: thank you for reading.

—*Bradley Olson*
August, 2023

Myth and the Calendar

Valentine's Day
(FEBRUARY 14, 2017)

The origins of Valentine's Day are a bit murky, but they seem to reach back far into the early Roman celebrations of Romulus and Remus and the fertility festival of Lupercalia celebrated at the ides of February, the fifteenth of February. Lupercalia was itself a modification of another, even older (dating back to Etruscan or Sabine cultures) springtime cleansing ritual, Februa, which lent its name to the month of the year. Later, as Christianity was emerging in the empire, there were several Christian martyrs named Valentine or Valentinus in the first few centuries of the early church. One of them, perhaps even all of them, were remembered in the celebration of a feast day named in their honor and situated on the fourteenth of February; the familiar modus operandi of the Christian Church to co-opt venerable pagan celebrations, rename them, and redefine them in Christian terms in order to make the new celebration seems familiar to pagans and facilitates a broader acceptance of Christianity.

I am particularly fond of one legend that describes an imprisoned, and doubtless soon to be martyred, Valentine sending a greeting of love to a young girl with whom he fell in love while he was incarcerated. He signed the missive, "From your Valentine." Not only is this a sweet story explaining the continued use of the phrase, but it also points out the rather painful aspects of love—I recall Joseph Campbell remarking in *A Joseph Campbell Companion* that romantic love is an ordeal—aspects one would rather overlook in exchange for contemplating the more exhilarating, self-affirming, blissful aspects of love. Loving another, and communicating that love, is often not easy, especially if the thrilling, enthralling, novelty of love has settled into a predictable familiarity, and perhaps just such a communication is something that Valentine's Day affords.

Among the modern symbols and images of Valentine's Day, one in particular stands out: the honeybee-winged infant, Eros, clumsily holding his wee bow and tiny arrows that, if one of them found its mark, the target wouldn't notice as anything more than the sting of a mosquito. This image of Eros—infantile, small, impotent, speechless, dependent, and incapable of adult, especially sexual, relationships—may well represent an unconscious, neurotic orientation to love that is gaged by the value of the gifts bestowed and the hackneyed, greeting-card folderol that passes for poetry, and alerts us to the fact that, culturally speaking, we don't want to work too hard at love.

Compare the Valentine's Day Eros to the Eros depicted in ancient Greek culture: Eros was among the oldest of the gods, fully mature, robust, and muscular, bearing angelic golden wings and, as sculpted by Praxiteles, heartrendingly beautiful. Hesiod, in his *Theogony*, writes that it's the influence of Eros, of love, that first gives form to the universe. His arrows also wound and thereby give form to the human heart. Sometimes they kindle love, and sometimes they cause an aversion to the beloved. Even the greatest of the gods were not immune to his influence. This Eros is hardly a powerless child, and one must wonder how ideas of love would change if this were the image of Eros we faced each February 14. One encounters in the Eros of Hesiod and Praxiteles the often disorienting, disturbing nature of the sublime, and the difficult pleasures of the sublime are never more present than when one becomes vulnerable enough to love deeply, unhesitatingly, and wholeheartedly.

MAY *the* BLESSINGS
of ST. PATRICK BEHOLD YOU
(MARCH 7, 2017)

We are all familiar with the trope of St. Patrick driving the snakes out of Ireland, but the real St. Patrick was even more remarkable in real life than the pied piper we have come to know through such silliness as pinching and green beer on March 17 of each year. Patricius was kidnapped by Irish pirates sometime in the fifth century from his home in Great Britain when he was sixteen, taken to Ireland, where he became a shepherd-slave to an Irish chieftain, and charged with the bitterly lonely, excruciatingly hungry life of guarding his master's goats and sheep. He took this opportunity to return to his Christian faith, becoming something of a mystic. After six years of isolation and hardship, a mysterious dream voice told him, "Your hungers are rewarded; you are going home" (*Confessio*). He arose, made a long, treacherous journey to the Irish Sea, found passage on a ship, and sailed back to England. After finding himself comfortably at home and reunited with his family, he had yet another vision in which he is handed a "letter," the heading of which simply said *Vox Hiberionacum*, the voice of the Irish. He developed a desire to return to the *pagus*, the uncultivated Irish countryside, and walk among the *pagans* who, to civilized Romans such as Patricius's family, were uncivilized, unreliable, and threatening. He was ordained a priest and later a bishop, and became, in all probability, the first missionary bishop of the Roman Church.

Once he returned to Ireland, Patricius found that he loved Ireland and its people, so raucous and crude, and he referred to them lovingly as his "warrior children." So much did he love Ireland and the Irish that he became one of them. He identified himself as Irish and felt his Irishness down to the depths of his soul. And while he never did, in fact, drive the snakes out of Ireland, he did almost single handedly transform Ireland in other ways: he attacked the slave trade with a passion that only a former slave could possess, and by the end of his life (or shortly thereafter) slavery was no longer an undisputed reality. In fact, murders and other forms of violence that had once been commonplace in Ireland greatly declined.

The important thing for me, contemplating the life of Patricius, is not the mythology surrounding him: driving snakes out of Ireland, using a shamrock as a parable, or even his walking stick that grew into an ash tree. What's important to me is understanding that sometimes, while in the midst of living one's familiar, commonplace life, we can be abducted by our own life's purpose and subjected to hardship and grief. These violent psychological and sometimes physical tribulations, while presenting us with all sorts of problems, are perpetrated upon us by our own futurity, our own life's purpose or meaning reaching back to us, manhandling us, and roughly placing us upon our life's path. I don't think it would be wrong to think of this as the modus operandi of bliss.

The SAGACITY *of* FOOLS
(APRIL 4, 2017)

April 1, April Fools' Day, is a day traditionally set aside for playing tricks on people or hoaxing. Pranks and hoaxes range from the very clever, such as the BBC's spaghetti harvest or an article in the April 1998 issue of *New Mexicans for Science and Reason* suggesting that the Alabama legislature had decided that the value of pi should be changed from 3.14 to 3.0, bringing it closer to the "biblical value;" to the old, hackneyed pranks of gluing coins to sidewalks and replacing the creamy center of Oreo cookies with toothpaste. I suspect that the celebrations of hilarity and good humor are as old as humankind, but one of the earliest instances of specifically April foolery in the historical record was *poisson d'avril*, which dates back to the fifteenth century and includes attaching a paper fish to an unaware victim's back. A kind of medieval Kick Me sign, I suppose. April Fools' pranks may also have a dark side, it seems, and may smack a bit of humiliation and a smug manipulation of the credulous and the uncomplicated.

Those two qualities in particular, credulousness and an uncomplicated simplicity, constitute the heart of the fool. In the plays of Shakespeare, one finds any number of apparent simpletons who speak incisively and truthfully about the nature of life, of love, and of politics. Like Nick Bottom, fools are often possessed of a "most rare vision," a vision that makes sense of a mixed-up world, a world that has been turned upside down by greed, cruelty, and fear. The fool, in his nonsense, his glibness, his often slapstick manner, is able to speak truth uninhibitedly and frankly, thereby setting the world aright once more. By ridiculing the foolish, society's anxieties find an outlet in laughter as well as a welcome reassurance that one is not, oneself, a fool. But if one looks more deeply, one may find in foolishness a profound critique of the sociopolitical forces that conspire to make one foolish. The fool offers an effective critique of society because she understands existence experienced from the inside out rather than the socially sanctioned outside in. The fool is aware (and brings the fact into our awareness too) that those who judge her have never deeply examined their own lives and have no way of understanding *différance* except to call it foolishness or asinine.

Beneath the fool's unconventional, sometimes shocking, behavior, one finds a deep wisdom. Marie-Louise von Franz connected the fool with "a part of the personality, or even of humanity which remained behind and therefore still has the original wholeness of nature" (*Lectures on Jung's Typology*). In the Tarot deck, the fool is the first of the major arcana and bears the number zero. Zero first appeared in Egypt in the early second millennium BCE, and only found its way to Europe in the eleventh century. The concept of zero is a little mind-blowing in that it presents the apparent paradox of nothing being something, a nothing that actually occupies space. Zero is a whole, rational, real number that has power mathematically, denominatively, and even imaginally. When one considers zero's circular shape, one naturally imagines ideas such as totality, wholeness, and a universal, all-encompassing vessel within which everything is in harmonious relationship with everything else.

A fool, then, is well suited to take on the task of revealing truth, a project so fraught with danger and misunderstanding that who but a fool would propose to do such a thing? And the workshop of the fool, the place in which he conjures his particular reconciling, healing magic, is the human heart, the center of the empty circle. The fool's genius works for all of us, helping us understand that hidden in what appears to be nothing is a very important something. The fool moves us to understand this, and the fool's admonition to King Lear should challenge all of us too: "Can you make no use of nothing, nuncle?"

The REVOLUTION *of* SPRING
(MAY 2, 2017)

¡Feliz Cinco de Mayo! Cinco de Mayo is a day that marks the Battle of Puebla, first celebrated in California in the 1860s. Although commonly misunderstood, Cinco de Mayo is not the same as Mexican Independence Day, the national holiday celebrated later in the year on September 16. At the Battle of Puebla, a much-stronger French force was demolished by a small, poorly armed Mexican force, a remarkable feat given that in 1861 the French were considered to be the greatest military force in the world. This Mexican victory reinvigorated a flagging resistance and sparked fierce patriotism in its ongoing fight for self-determination.

While Cinco de Mayo is not a national holiday in Mexico, it has become an enormously popular celebration of Mexican-American culture in the United States. And with good reason: the US owes its present configuration to Mexico's May 5 victory because, if the French had not been so badly beaten at Puebla, they would most certainly have entered the American Civil War on the side of the Confederacy, drastically reversing the balance of power and altering the destiny of the US. But Cinco de Mayo is not only a Mexican-American celebration; in various forms it has migrated around the world. Canada, Jamaica, Australia, and New Zealand all hold Cinco de Mayo celebrations. Europe, South Africa, Nigeria, and even Japan host May 5 celebrations of Latin American culture.

Harbored deep in the soul of political revolution is the idea of autonomy, that human beings possess natural, unalienable rights of which they shall not be deprived by governments or by agreements between governments. The foremost of these human rights acknowledges that human beings must be independent and free. In many ways, I think this idea of human freedom is the *conditio sine qua non*, the fundamental subject with which myth wrestles. Regardless of setting, regardless of epoch or era, regardless of culture, the fundamental question of myth becomes how a human being finds freedom and to what degree they may actually be free.

It is often remarked that freedom is a terrible and burdensome responsibility, and as such it's often refused. What makes genuine freedom overwhelming, in large part, is the anguish accompanying it: the anguish of forced choices in the face of uncertainty and ignorance, anguish over the consequences (intended or not) of our decisions, and, most of all, anguish over the imperative, the human responsibility, to create our own existence when there is plenty of anecdotal, longitudinal evidence that suggests we can't. Nowhere is anguish better dramatized than in the tragedies of Sophocles, Aeschylus, and Euripides, who famously lamented "in childbirth grief begins."

It's not an accident, I think, that in spring a people's thoughts may turn to revolution. The breaking up and turning over of earth to herald new life can't fail to inspire thoughts of overthrowing oppressors, autocrats, or absolutisms. So many revolutionary acts occurred in springtime: the battles of Lexington and Concord, the Arab Spring, May Revolutions in France and Argentina, and, strikingly, the Revolutions of 1848 across Europe and known variously as People's Spring, Spring of Nations, and Springtime of the Peoples. In springtime, there is also a call to personal revolution, to live a new life that is richer, deeper, and somehow more meaningful. Revolutions, as Marx suggested, may well be the locomotives of history, but personal revolutions are the locomotives of living.

The GODDESS, BEAUTIFUL *in* TEARS
(MAY 23, 2017)

As I watch the renewing, generative energies of spring wrestle with the lingering grip of winter in the mountains of Northern Arizona, it might be apt to remember Freyja, the most familiar and powerful of the Norse goddesses, whose beneficent influence in the concerns of love, beauty (particularly gold), and fertility was popularly sought after. She is a conspicuous figure in *the Poetic Edda*, the sagas of great tragic poetry from which J. R. R. Tolkien drew inspiration, which were compiled and set down from older traditional sources in 1000 to 1300 AD.

Freyja is the most glorious of the Norse goddesses and the most kindly disposed to humankind. She's particularly fond of lovers, and mediates disputes between mortals and gods alike. When she travels, she is carried in a chariot pulled by two cats. Another remarkable mode of transportation for Freyja is her cloak of feathers, which she often loans to other gods, notably Loki and Thor, to aid them in their efforts. In the *Eddas* (a prose *Edda* also exists, written in the late thirteenth century and attributed to Snorri Sturluson), there are many commentaries on Freyja's beauty as well as her generative powers. She is described as flying over the earth sprinkling morning dew as spring flowers fall from her hair and, in a trope made famous by poets, weeping tears that turn to gold. Many plants in Scandinavia were named for her (Freyja's Tears and Freyja's Hair are familiar examples), and despite being reduced in rank during the process of Christianization, Freyja continues to be influential in Scandinavian folklore and art to this day.

I think one may attribute her enduring popularity to the sense that there is something quite modern, as well as something necessary to modern life, about Freyja, something indomitable, civilizing, and empowering to be found in her strength, her compassion, and her wisdom. Because of the mysterious loss of her husband, Freyja is overcome by sorrow, crying tears which, when fallen to the earth, turn to gold, a precious gift to humans that suggests that even though one's grief may be profound, one may still offer comfort and beauty to others and the world.

Freyja's strategic martial and political gifts seem essential in creating balance and restraint in the midst of her often hot-tempered Aesirian brethren. Her spirit may easily be reimagined at work in contemporary life, attending to issues of poverty, domestic violence, illiteracy, sanitation, food supply, and reproductive and human rights. She might have even found herself at the forefront of a movement that has proved to be the most efficacious way to rapidly raise the quality of life in countries affected by prolonged conflict, abysmal health care, and profound poverty: the empowerment of women.

When women are empowered in developing nations, communities bloom. They flower for the simple, logical reason that the act of integrating half of a community's members back into the life of a society doubles the available talent, brainpower, and wisdom, and vastly increases community commitment. In such a situation, all the community's members have a chance to become more educated, more dignified, and more humane, no longer living lives of mere subsistence and survival. Self-expression, innovation, art, social reciprocity, practical reason, and conviviality—all those things that make human beings value being human—begin to flourish, and the nobility of all humans shines through. Individuals begin to hope again, have goals, aspirations, activities, and plans, thereby overturning the old ideas that previously regarded people as pawns or property serving another's ends and casting such prejudices in an abhorrent light.

In her book *Women and Human Development*, the philosopher Martha Nussbaum writes that "fully human functioning requires affiliation and reciprocity with others," and affiliation and reciprocity are surely among the most highly developed of Freyja's values.

Juno: Not Everyone Knows How *to* Love *the* Terrifying, Strange, *or* Beautiful

(JUNE 6, 2017)

As we enter the month of June, we remember that this month, her birth month, is named for Juno, the Roman goddess married to her brother Jupiter, the goddess who has traditionally been concerned with all aspects of women's lives. Not an easy responsibility at any time or in any place in the world. Her resume speaks to her many skills: Juno was a powerful military goddess, and she seems to have had oracular powers, as was suggested by one of her names, Juno Moneta (the verb *monere* means to warn, hence Juno the Warner). She is a tremendously complex figure, and this complexity, coupled with the great accumulation of epithets she's acquired, suggests to me a goddess of great age and influence. She is, for example, mentioned with Hercules in an inscription consecrating the Temple of Hercules at Lanuvium, a very ancient site, and it appears the two of them together assisted women and infants in the perilous proposition of childbirth. In the Greek tradition, they are bound together in a difficult, contentious relationship.

One epithet I find particularly compelling is Juno Lucina, who, in her relationship to the moon represents the cyclical, renewing nature of cosmic time, just as the menstrual cycle articulates cycles of biological time. Generally speaking, it's safe to say that goddesses who are associated with the moon are also associated with some aspect of childbirth. Her role in renewing time puts her in a relationship to Janus, who presided over the passage of time from the previous to the subsequent month. Some scholars suggest that Juno's original spouse was Janus, not Jupiter. Juno and Janus seem to have much more in common, and perhaps if that relationship had survived, Juno would have been a much more happily married goddess.

In Juno/Hera's mirthless, troubled marriage, one finds the mythic mirror reflecting contemporary truths about gender roles and relationships between wives and husbands. Had she been mortal, I'm sure she would have been among the first in line to buy and read Betty Friedan's *The Feminine Mystique* when it was first published:

> The problem lay buried, unspoken, for many years in the minds of . . . women. It was a strange stirring, a sense of dissatisfaction, a yearning. . . . Each [woman] struggled with it alone. As she [went about the mundane tasks of her daily existence] she was afraid to ask even of herself the silent question—"Is this all (p.13)?"

Hera seems to me the most humanlike of the gods, not just in her frustrations and regrets but especially in her deep longing and considerable aspiration. Unlike her profligately promiscuous husband, she was scrupulous in her refusal to dishonor marital fidelity, and she's repaid for that loyalty by living in myth as a harridan, a shrew, a competitive battle-ax who wants nothing more than to control her hard-working and hard-playing husband. We tend to be unable to see behind her frustration to the deep wound she carries, a wound that contemporary human beings should recognize as a metaphor for human existence.

Hera received her wound, Homer tells us, when Herakles struck her in the right breast with an arrow. If we can read symbolically, and therefore mythically, the wound in her breast and its periodic relationship to the moon suggests an incurable wound to the feminine that seems at times to be nonexistent yet, at other times, inflicts unimaginable agony. This is also an apt description of her psychological suffering. Juno was admired, envied, lusted after, betrayed, humiliated, and abused until she was sick of it, and she lashed out in a bitter, all-too-human way. Juno's existence is defined by her wound. She's condemned to an existentially dreadful, one might say incurable, existence due to her immortality. Human dread is the other side of the existential coin; we cannot be cured from our mortality, and so we share with her an unbreakable bond forged by the existential dread of an incurable and inevitable wound.

So perhaps we might have more empathy for Juno, the benefactress we've never recognized or wanted, perhaps because her suffering is so humanlike that the idea of her, rather than distracting or comforting us, makes the wound of our own mortality all the more difficult to bear. And in our expression of empathy for the suffering goddess, we just might find some for ourselves.

INDEPENDENCE *and* HANGING TOGETHER
(JULY 4, 2017)

In the United States, July 4 is a national holiday celebrating the Second Continental Congress's approval of the Declaration of Independence, a document created to explain Congress's decision on July 2, 1776 to formally separate from British rule and form an independent nation composed of the original thirteen colonies. John Adams believed it would be July 2 that would be celebrated in American memory "from this time forward forever more." But in the American creation myth, the founding fathers signed the declaration on July 4, even though most historians believe the Declaration of Independence was signed much later, perhaps even a month later, on August 2.

Initially, when fighting began in 1775, Americans were fighting only for their rights as British subjects, and all out war with Great Britain was not an option anyone relished. Yet in another year the revolution was under way, and congressional action resulting in the issuance of the Declaration of Independence had been taken. The war was costly, both in blood and treasure; casualty rates were second only to the Civil War. Americans banded together to fight a capriciously tyrannical monarchy and "mutually pledge to each other," as Jefferson wrote in the declaration, "our Lives, our Fortunes and our sacred Honor." There are few government-generated documents that transcend their functions as forms, records, certificates, authorizations, or policy, and actually live. The Declaration of Independence is one such living document; it seems sentient and discursive, at times angry, disappointed, insulted, and anxious. But above all it seems determined to extract an enduring pledge of justice, safety, happiness, and prudence for its citizens while simultaneously encouraging Americans to live a meaningful life. In return, the pledge from each of us is that we will give our best and our all to every person engaged in this bold, risky, and ultimately fragile experiment, that we make a commitment to one another as well as the nation, to continue to breathe life into that most remarkable of documents, a document which shall continually need to be resuscitated by every new generation of Americans.

I think nothing is better at emphasizing the glaring discrepancy between individual perceptions and desires and the harsh inflexibility of external reality than mythology. The ability of myth to highlight injustice and sniff out hypocrisy may certainly be brought to bear on the lives of nation-states as well. While the concept of a state is reasonably clear and objectively defined—it's a necessary organizing principle—a nation is different. A nation is a mythological, imaginal notion, a living personification of a mythical concept.

Jefferson's Declaration of Independence was a pronouncement of individual freedom, and as such it is the first attempt at shaping and advancing the founding mythology of America. In contemporary life we can see the discrepancies, as well as the fault lines, between aspiration and reality, between individuality and plurality, but only a little more than a decade after the declaration, the United States Constitution emphasized the words "We the people" and "a more perfect union." Perhaps the best measure of independence is the recognition that I am interdependent rather than independent, that I am that much freer when I work to ensure that those immortal words—life, liberty, and the pursuit of happiness—apply to each and every American.

ECLIPSE: IN DARKNESS
ONE FINDS *the* LIGHT
(AUGUST 22, 2017)

Yesterday, on August 21, Americans living within the umbral cone had a ringside seat to the latest total solar eclipse that was, for the first time in twenty-six years, visible in the US. As you know, a solar eclipse occurs when the moon passes between the earth and the sun, minimizing the bright sunlight of the day. Because of their relative distance and size, when it is closest to the earth the moon appears large enough to completely cover the sun, creating a few minutes of uncommon, otherworldly duskiness on an otherwise sunlit day. Umbraphiles from all over the world will travel to various places within the US to position themselves in the direct path of the eclipse. Solar eclipses are not all that unusual (averaging one totality, somewhere on Earth, every eighteen months), but to witness a total solar eclipse at the exact same location, one would have to wait about 375 years.

The Chinese were ingenious astronomers and began keeping records of eclipses around 720 BCE. Shi Shen predicted eclipses based on the relative positions of the sun and moon as early as the fourth century BCE. By and large, though, eclipses have not always provoked cool, rational, scientific inquiry. We get the word *eclipse* from the Greek word *ekleipsis*, which means abandonment, and often during an eclipse, when daylight had seemed to abandon them, people reacted with fear and panic, regarding eclipses as bad omens or ill portents. One may imagine that the disruption of the natural order—night falling in the middle of the day—was a cause for real concern.

A surprising number of cultures created mythologies of an animal of some kind swallowing the sun. Mayan paintings show a giant serpent swallowing the sun, for the Chinese it was a dragon, and for people living in the region of Hungary a bird was responsible. In southern Siberia a bear swallowed the sun, while in Southeast Asia a toad or frog was the culprit. In Norse mythology, a wolf named Skoll steals the sun with the intention to eat it, and local residents make as much noise as possible to scare Skoll away from his feast.

There are other mythological motifs to explain the disappearance of the sun too. For example, in some African myths the sun and moon are fighting during an eclipse. In some North American indigenous eclipse myths, the sun and the moon marry, and given that stars and planets are visible during an eclipse, the solar-lunar romance results in the birth of other heavenly objects.

Misunderstandings of the nature and power of eclipses have even persisted into the modern era as evidenced by the surprisingly common belief that an eclipse is dangerous to pregnant women and may cause birth defects in unborn children. Fears attend the upcoming eclipse too, although perhaps less fantastical in nature. People fear shortages of food, water, bathrooms, and gasoline due to tourists flooding into communities along the path of the totality. One researcher even suggested that eclipse mania in these parts of the country will resemble a "zombie apocalypse."

Admittedly, I haven't seen the morning news yet, but I doubt that there will have been a zombie apocalypse. But it does illustrate the great difficulty we humans have dealing with experiences that seem to subvert the natural order of things, of events that trigger a primal feeling within us that unusual powers are at work. To explain those moments, we then create narratives wherein the distinction between imagination and reality are erased, as when something that we have hitherto regarded as imaginary or impossible appears before us in reality. It is then we discover that those primitive fears, of which we are so confident we've overcome, seem once more to be activated. It is then that we rely on the power of myth to deal with the production of the existential anxiety from which the majority of us human beings have never quite managed to free ourselves.

The Giver *of* Gifts
Who Destroys Obstacles
(AUGUST 29, 2017)

This year, Ganesha's birthday is celebrated in the Hindu month of *Bhadrapada*, which on the Gregorian calendar falls on August 23 A festival of celebration, called a *Chaturthi*, lasts for eleven days and ends on September 5.

Ganesha is commonly referred to as "the remover of obstacles" and is among the most popular of the Hindu gods. He is a favorite household deity in India, and his popularity and acceptance are remarkable, particularly since he comes, apparently quite literally out of nowhere, around the fourth or fifth century CE (and of course, there is debate as to just how old Ganesha is), beginning to appear in the late texts of the *Puranas* around 600 CE. Perhaps that shouldn't be too surprising, since we often experience solutions to problems or obstacles as "coming out of nowhere." Being a favorite god of traders and therefore sailors, Ganesha traveled widely and became popular in Indonesia, Southeast Asia, China, Japan, and even reaching into pre-Islamic Afghanistan. Ganesha's skills in obstacle removal have frequently been called upon, and during colonialism, he provided a rallying point for the Indian people against British imperialism and aided in India's successful efforts to recover self-rule.

Images of Ganesha depict him with the body of a man and the head of an elephant, symbolism which depicts the unity of the microcosm (humans) and the macrocosm (the universe). The human body of Ganesha represents the manifest principle, inferior to the unmanifest or immaterial realm symbolized by the elephant's head. Ganesha has a mouse as a companion, which probably symbolizes his ability to penetrate, mouselike, through and to the most secret and hidden places. It's not uncommon that when one uncovers, or becomes conscious of the most hidden, secret places within oneself, obstacles melt away or even become transformed into opportunities. Certainly, size is a concept one cannot escape when contemplating the images of Ganesha, the immensity of the elephant and the tininess of the rat; it's almost as if, in the iconic representations of Ganesha, one might see into the deep nature of the universe: vast yet simultaneously atomic. Of course, Ganesha is often depicted with many arms and a massive belly, features which represent the infinite abundance of compassion that he possesses for other beings.

In addition to being the remover of obstacles, in his manifestation as *Ganapati*, he is the Lord of Categories, embodying everything the mind can grasp. All that can be counted or comprehended is a category, or *gana*, and, simply put, a category is a collection of things. In his book *The Myths and Gods of India*, Alain Daniélou writes, "The principle of all the classifications through which the relations between different orders of things, between the macrocosm and the microcosm, can be understood is called the lord-of-categories (Ganapati)." Among other things, the Lord of Categories is a scholar, a patron of schools, a writer, and a scribe, and to him it is attributed the recording of the *Mahabharata*, one of the two major Sanskrit epics.

The relationships between the microcosm and the macrocosm comprise nearly the whole region of concern in religion and philosophy; the effort toward reconciling the material with the immaterial, the known with the unknown, is the defining human enterprise. No wonder humans admire Ganapati, that theriocephalic genius of the Ganapati Upanishad who, in his categorical knowledge of everything, becomes "the giver of gifts who destroys obstacles."

THE FORTUNATE FALL
(OCTOBER 17, 2017)

In *Anne of Green Gables*, L. M. Montgomery wrote, "I'm so glad I live in a world where there are Octobers." I understand her sentiment: oaks, maples, sumac are everywhere ablaze, and the morning air is crisp enough to invigorate but not yet cold enough to drive one back inside. Animals are busy preparing for winter, their preparations important enough that this time of year they don't mind being watched by fascinated humans. Fall is beautiful everywhere I've ever experienced it, and yet fall has always made me sad, made my hope a rather fragile thing. I relate more to Hemingway, who wrote in *A Moveable Feast*:

> You expected to be sad in the fall. Part of you died each year when the leaves fell from the trees and their branches were bare against the wind and the cold, wintery light. But you knew there would always be the spring, as you knew the river would flow again after it was frozen. When the cold rains kept on and killed the spring, it was as though a young person died for no reason.

And when those cold rains continue to fall, one may well be comforted by the consoling power of myths.

As you may already know, Joseph Campbell posited four functions of myth, the second of which is called the cosmological function, and it serves to illustrate and explain aspects of the natural world as well as, to some degree, the universe itself. For instance, a Huron legend tells of a deer and a bear who passed over the Rainbow Bridge and into the Sky Land, where they fought. During a fierce and long battle, the bear's flesh was torn by the sharp, cruel horns of the deer, and they both fled along the paths of the sky as the wolf arrived to break up the fight. As the deer ran, drops of the bear's blood fell from his horns into the lower world, turning the leaves of trees scarlet, yellow, crimson, and brown. The Huron say that each year the blood of the bear is once again thrown down from the sky onto the trees. The cosmological function of mythology is an attempt to explain why the world is as it is, or perhaps more importantly why we experience it as we do.

To that end, the last of Campbell's four functions is the psychological. Myths read through a psychological lens help us understand the unfolding of human existence, the challenge of living life with integrity, greater self-awareness, compassion, and community. When Hemingway wrote, "Part of you died each year when the leaves fell," he is relating a cosmological truth to a psychological one; the death of hope, the sense of running out of time, and a colder, darker world are all sentiments psychologically apropos to the fall season. Fall is a reminder that even the most beautiful, the most vibrant life ends. Life's brevity is like autumn's brevity; if these were not brief, would they be as beautiful? Autumn is a time of richness, of fullness, and it is the year's last and loveliest reminder of just how beautiful this world is.

Fall creates a kind of liminal space in which, nearly simultaneously, we must hold the whole of our own life's most brilliantly colorful expressions as well as the knowledge that it will soon end—and it *always* ends too soon. And that it ends is right and proper, and suitable for humankind. Such an awareness coming, I hope, before one's last brittle, shrunken, palsied leaf falls from the tree of life is perhaps one of the most meaningful realizations of a life lived following bliss.

Writing Myth:
The Mythopoetics of
Mythic Literature,
Psychology, and Philosophy

I believe that psychology, art, literature, and cultural studies lend understanding and relevance to myth, just as myth lends understanding and relevance to psychology, art, literature, and cultural studies. This essential reciprocity moves one's understanding toward a deep relationship with beauty, the fascinating mystery of existence, with dignity and creativity—in short, with life itself. The following essays focus on the reciprocity and interdependence between myth and other related domains.

THE AFFLICTIONS *of* PHILOCTETES: THE WORK *of* SOME RUDE HAND

It seems to me that life on this planet displays a disturbing propensity for the powerful to further afflict the already afflicted. The personae non gratae, the sick, the powerless, and the poor are forced to live in the margins of a society from which they've been ostracized. Not surprisingly, the temptation to punch down seems to be an atavistic and apparently ineradicable strain of human nature, which Sophocles addresses in his tragedy from 409 BCE titled, simply, *Philoctetes*. Sophocles was the defender and patron of those whom society had tossed aside and wrote movingly about betrayal, abandonment, and the last moral voice standing in opposition to unprincipled leaders or overwhelming force.

Philoctetes was already famous for assisting Hercules to die, when the latter suffered brutally from the diabolical Nessus's poisoned shirt. For this compassionate act, Philoctetes became renowned for his loyalty in friendship, and the heir to Hercules's bow and arrows, a Bronze-Age weapon of mass destruction. He was among the Argive armada sailing to Troy when they stopped at a tiny island along the way to sacrifice to a local deity, and it was then that Philoctetes was bitten by a snake. His groans of pain make the performance of the ritual impossible, spoiled by the ill-omened sounds of agony. Additionally, Philoctetes's wound began to suppurate and emit such a horribly foul odor that he was abandoned on a nearby deserted island, where he spent the next ten years in tremendous pain and suffering: "On every side I looked, and nothing saw but woe."

Eventually, the Argives learn they can defeat Troy only with the aid of Hercules's bow and arrows, and, presumably, that means they needed Philoctetes as well, as he was the owner of the weapons. They also learn that Achilles's son Neoptolemus must be summoned, given his father's armor, and help secure from their present owner the unsurpassable Herculean armaments. Neoptolemus and Odysseus set out to retrieve the bow of Hercules, but Odysseus had no intention of returning with Philoctetes, and was intent only on gaining the bow through deceit, trickery, or force. Initially, cunning Odysseus convinced Neoptolemus to work with him to deceive Philoctetes. But the more Neoptolemus watched Philoctetes gallantly bear his hideous wound, his betrayal, and suffering, the more he realized he could not treat this noble soul, whom he had come to love, so shabbily. Neoptolemus decided he would lie no longer, told Philoctetes about their mission to defraud him, and returned to him the bow and arrows of Hercules, an act of honesty and atonement that enraged Odysseus but further endeared Neoptolemus to Philoctetes. After some hesitation Philoctetes eventually agreed to return to Troy with Neoptolemus and Odysseus after a too-tidy deus ex machina intervention by Hercules (who, after his death, became a god), directed Philoctetes to return to Troy, win the war and be healed of his wound by the sons of Asclepius.

All the ruined, broken-yet-unbowed heroes of Sophocles's greatest plays—*Ajax*, *Oedipus at Colonus*, and *Philoctetes*—remain, against all odds, people of remarkable virtue. It is a virtue made all the more remarkable by their humiliating circumstances, and the reader is left with no alternative but to admire them. Because of their ghastly suffering, they no longer have regard for the demands or opinions of others; they are, in a moral sense, entirely free. It is the nature of the powerful like Odysseus to focus solely on those things that materially serve their power, while they choose to disregard values, humanity, and pathos.

The powerful overlook marginalized people like Philoctetes: invalids, the desperately needy, the most disenfranchised—those human beings Fortuna's wheel has rolled by or, alternatively, run right over. Dissolving the deontological divide between Philoctetes and Odysseus is the guileless, humane young man who sees another not as a means to an end but as a fellow human being whose suffering elicits empathy and whose dignity elicits love. To think generously and kindly toward others, not acting as though people are tools to be employed for naked self-interest, is our charge. If we fail in this charge, then as Philoctetes said, "I dread the woes to come; for well I know when once the mind's corrupted it brings forth unnumbered crimes, and ill to ills succeed."

THE POWER *of the* FLEETING APPARITION

This week I want to explore the uses of myth. The uses of myth are abundant, and they exert influences in every aspect of human life, "galvanizing populations, creating civilizations, each with a beauty and self-compelling destiny of its own" (Joseph Campbell, *The Masks of God, Volume 1: Primitive Mythology*). Mythologies are very powerful things indeed. Myth has the power to acquaint one with the vastness and complexity of the universe, to inspire transcendent awareness, but it also has the power to shrink and domesticate the universe, reduce it to a familiar, bounded space in which human beings live comfortably and, too often perhaps, smugly in the knowledge that the universe was made for us. It needs human beings (and special, chosen ones at that) in order to exist.

Campbell recognized the dangers of literalizing myth and believing in it as though it were an incontestable fact:

> Clearly mythology is no toy for children. . . . For its symbols (whether in the tangible form of images or in the abstract form of ideas) touch and release the deepest centers of motivation, moving literate and illiterate alike, moving mobs, moving civilizations. . . . For surely it is folly to preach to children who will be riding rockets to the moon a morality and a cosmology based on concepts of the Good Society and of man's place in nature that were coined before the harnessing of the horse! And the world is now far too small, and men's stake in sanity too great, for any more of these old games of chosen folk . . . by which

tribesmen were sustained against their enemies in the days when the serpent still could talk (p.12).

Roland Barthes, in his brilliant and provocative book *Mythologies*, argued that myth is "a system of communication, that it is a message. This allows one to perceive that myth cannot possibly be an object, a concept, or an idea; it is a mode of signification, a form" (p. 109). For Barthes the message of myth consists of material (oral or written narrative, art, photography, cinema, music) that has already been worked on, sometimes over many centuries, to make incredibly effective communications.

The message of myth signifies a particular state of consciousness with which one may enter into, explore, discuss, or dissect without attending to its substance (to be clear, that is not the same as saying the substance of a myth is unimportant). On this particular point, at least, Barthes seems to be in accord with Campbell in the sense that the form of myth insists upon metaphor, a communication more plastic, more flexible, more mercurial than literal, factual objects can be.

Myth is, for me at least, most meaningful when one explores the deeper messages the myths suggest. Those messages don't lend themselves to literal or factual understanding, and we always end up by saying what they are like. This is not a shortcoming at all, and the immersion into the message—sometimes confusing or incomprehensible—is itself participation in the powerfully primal rhythms of life, our own as well as the life of the world. Ludwig Wittgenstein once suggested that the limits of one's world are defined by the limits of one's language, and I sense that at one's limits or edges, a protean potential for changes of mind, thought, and feeling—a radical deconstruction of perspective—is present. It's the challenge of working at the limits or the edges of oneself, and one's limited ability to speak about it, that unearths important awareness and deep truths.

To discover the true power of myth, it must not, I believe, be worked within the confines of that which one finds comfortable, established, or understandable; those qualities never move us closer to boundaries or limits. It is difficult, however, to prevent the exploration of myth from lapsing into the literal and the comfortable, becoming nothing more than a comforting fantasy. I think there should be an element of danger as one works with metaphor and myth. Not physical danger, obviously, but rather an element of psychological danger in the sense that one is courting awarenesses that, once realized, may bring one to one's knees, subvert one's ego and its perceptions of the self, and perhaps even radically change one's life. No, myth is certainly not a tool for children, nor is it made for childish adults. To quote Mephistopheles in Goethe's *Faust*, "The very best that thou dost know / Thou dar'st not to the striplings show."

Bliss *is* Not Found *in* Faithfulness *to* Forms, But *in* Liberation *from* Them

I've been thinking a lot about the theme of independence, reflecting on Joseph Campbell's often bold, independent nature and what it means to become an independent human being. As Campbell describes in *Pathways to Bliss*, independence is a difficult achievement for humans:

> The first fact that distinguishes the human species from all others is that we are born too soon. We arrive, incapable of taking care of ourselves for something like fifteen years. Puberty doesn't come along for twelve years or more, and physical maturity doesn't arrive until our early twenties. During the greater part of this long arc of life, the individual is in a psychological situation of dependency. We are trained, as children, so that every stimulus, every experience, leads us simply to react, "Who will help me?"

The reflexive, human reaction to novelty and fear, to the unfamiliar or unknown is to ask, at least initially, "Who will help me?" Of course, the slowly dawning realization occurs that it is primarily oneself upon which one must rely, and this awful awareness is the beginning of maturity. In our maturity others may still point the way or render aid, they may still give comfort, but ultimately one understands that one has the solitary, and frequently heavy, responsibility to reach out, to investigate, or seek counsel, to deal with and navigate life's challenges. It's a challenge made all the more difficult because, as a rule, others no longer magically appear unbidden, as ideal parents may once have, and just when they were most needed. This is fundamentally how one grows and matures, and navigating this new reality is how one becomes an independent person.

Such a move toward maturity and independence is equally important in relation to our myths as well. Generally speaking, people believe that the objects of myth are somewhere "out there," either in this world or in some adjacent, perhaps ancient, unapproachable, or misapprehended realm. "Now," Campbell writes, "it's a basic mythological principle, I would say, that what is referred to in mythology as 'the other world' is really (in psychological terms) 'the inner world.' And what is spoken of as 'future' is 'now.'" Later he notes, "the incarnation—the avatar—is merely the model through which you find this miracle in yourself."

Ideally, one works to destroy the notion that the objects of mythic awe are somewhere out there, separate from oneself, while simultaneously discovering that one is, in fact, the thing one is searching for. It's a bit of a paradox, isn't it? We unconsciously create the objects of myth, project them out into the world so that they seem separate, perhaps even alien, from ourselves, and yet in some sense the objects of myth were there all along, within and without, waiting to be created, projected, and consciously realized.

The revolutionary change from dependence to independence in mythical thought is a substantive change from an orientation of mere relationship to an orientation of use. One shifts from a relational modality which simply places one in relationship to something other, something out there, to a perspective of use which gives the objects of myth energy, gravity, and presence within. One might say that the objects of myth are present-to-hand or ready-to-hand, and waiting to be put to use. Such a perspectival shift requires that the mythic idea, concept, or symbol experienced as other be reinterpreted and reconfigured in order to realize that one possesses these energies oneself. Destruction of the mythic symbols existing out there in the other world leads to the discovery of the symbol's deeper reality living within. Which is why, as the old saying goes, if you meet the Buddha on the road, you're encouraged to kill him. By understanding the objects of myth through the recognition of them as projections or fantasies, the reality of what they represent may be directly experienced in one's inner world. The iconoclastic move, the smashing of the image, results in the creation of a new space, both inner and outer, and a new reality that is no longer a mere potential or a fantasy, but an area of actual experience. This is why Campbell can say, responding to Bill Moyers's statement about him being a man of faith, "No, I don't have to have faith, I have experience (*The Power of Myth*, 208)."

The importance of this willing destruction cannot be overstated. It represents a birth into a living reality. From what was formerly a simplistic, dualistic concept or heuristic device, this move allows one to experience in a given moment a firsthand, transcendent reality of bliss and not merely the products of projective psychic processes. It enables myth to be *used*.

THE RADIANT,
REORDERING FORCE *of* ART

In a 1907 letter to his wife, Clara (a fine artist and sculptor in her own right, who had studied with, among others, Auguste Rodin), Rainer Maria Rilke wrote, "Only as though with their radiance can things reach us, and just as the magnet rouses and organises the forces in something susceptible to it, so they, through their influence, create within us a new ordering" (*The Selected Letters of Rainer Maria Rilke*, 121). Like art, the potential of myth to facilitate the creation of a new inner order is perhaps the primary reason behind Joseph Campbell's lifelong love of and scholarly fascination with myth and its relationship to the human psyche. In his work *The Ecstasy of Being*, releasing this month as an e-book, Campbell asserts, "In a work of proper art every aesthetic element has a psychological value equivalent to that of some mythological image or idea," and I think that the psychological value accompanying the mythological image is often one of ecstasy.

Ecstasy is derived from the Greek word *ekstasis*, which literally means to be standing outside of oneself, to be carried beyond individual, rational thought to a psychosomatic state in which rationality and personal volition are suspended. *Ekstasis* dissolves the sense of the bounded, the contained, the self-inspecting and self-experiencing sensation of the world and plunges one into a transcendent experience, an experience of the world, the universe even, as unified, timeless, unbounded, and harmonious.

Several years ago I was in the Metropolitan Museum of Art with the intent to enjoy the Greek and Roman wing of the museum when, finding myself with time on my hands, I wandered into the modern art section and was gobsmacked by a six-and-a-quarter-foot-tall, eighteen-and-a-half-foot-wide work of art by Anselm Kiefer called "Bohemia Lies by the Sea." I've since learned that Kiefer is a German artist born in 1945 and an author of several books. His body of work wrestles with recent German history such as Nazi rule, the Holocaust, and other controversial, sometimes even taboo, issues.

The ecstasy I experienced looking at this piece was no doubt abetted by its composition—a thickly painted oil, powdered paint, charcoal, shellac, emulsion on burlap—and three-dimensional quality. But even more affecting were the qualities of the artwork that didn't initially register in my conscious awareness during the initial viewing. The title, for instance, very subtly confuses or disequilibrates as one struggles with the thought, Bohemia doesn't lie by the sea at all, does it? I've always associated it with Prague, landlocked in Eastern Europe. And is that a hint of the sea at the top of the painting, or is it sky? Where does that road take me? All my associations to Bohemia, even the ideals of Bohemia were activated: Puccini's opera; the Broadway play *Rent*; the ideals of free-thinking, experimental art; and free love. The idea of Bohemia invokes a vigorously energetic and spirited, impecunious and thread-worn existence cloaking a richly baroque intellectual and spiritual life lived in a vaguely communal coalition of artists, intellectuals, and marginalized souls drawn together by a common utopian dream. Later still, I learned of the poem "Bohemia Lies by the Sea" by Ingeborg Bachmann (*Darkness Spoken: Collected Poems of Ingeborg Bachmann*, 2006.) which almost certainly served as some inspiration for Kiefer's painting. Here's an excerpt from that poem:

If it's me, then it's anyone, for he's as worthy as me.
I want nothing more for myself. I want to go under.

Under—that means the sea, there I'll find Bohemia
   again.
From my grave, I wake in peace.
From deep down I know now, and I'm not lost.

Well, suffice it to say that I am unable to ever again leave the
Met without having at least a glimpse of this painting. Its aesthetic, its *ekstasis*-inducing power, remains with me still. As
Campbell put it, the image "synthesizes the 'pulse of life' with
the 'stillness of death,'" allowing one to see through the literal painting to a background of mystery normally occluded to
the eye, which is finally, he says, the function of both art and
mythology. The ecstatic experience is bigger than the momen-
tary real, bigger than the painful or unbearable elements of life;
it is somehow full of inner awakening and soothing validation.
When looking at proper art, we are turned toward the Outside,
but when we are most so, momentous things are happening
inside of us, things that we might not know how to describe or
name, things that put our mundane anxieties to shame. One
discovers one's true self living in a place that isn't on any map,
ineffably radiant and powerful, in an inner Utopia, a Bohemia
near the Sea.

The Magic *of* Timeless Tales

What tales are more timeless than those of the Matter of Britain, the thematic cycle containing the legends of King Arthur? For Joseph Campbell, the Grail legend, and particularly Wolfram's *Parzival* "is the great mythos of the modern European world." But the Arthurian cycle was not the only recognized cycle of the Middle Ages; in fact, two other commonly recognized cycles of the medieval age were called, the Matter of Rome, stories that centered on the life and adventures—adventures that were conflated with the Trojan War—of Alexander the Great, and the Matter of France, which contains the stories of the adventures of Charlemagne and his paladins. In addition, there were a number of other, noncyclical romances written by medieval authors, such as *Robert the Devil*, a personal favorite of mine, a story about a Norman knight (of whom legend says was the father of William the Conqueror) who discovers that he is the son of Satan.

One of the things that made Joseph Campbell a remarkable scholar and storyteller was his ability to contextualize and frame his writing in such a way that the reader (or the listener) is rewarded with deeper and deeper insights. For example, in the first chapter of *Romance of the Grail: The Magic and Mystery of Arthurian Myth*, he notes how Europe formed itself into something entirely new as the result of powerful forces brought to bear upon it from the East: "An Oriental religion swept into Europe with real force at the end of the fourth century—namely, Christianity." That simple statement delivers the plangent reminder that at one time Christianity was strangely alien to a European sensibility, and perhaps it remains unconsciously strange to modern ears (hence its enduring power to fascinate) because, as Campbell goes on to write, "A century or so later [after the establishment of Christianity as the state religion of the Roman Empire] the European portion of the Roman Empire collapsed and what we called Rome from then on is really Constantinople, which is Byzantium, which is Asia again."

Looking at even the most common of themes in the Arthurian tales, love for instance, forces us to recontextualize and rethink the stories with that in mind. Until roughly the twelfth century and the appearance of the troubadours and romance legends like *Parzival*, essentially two types of love existed in the traditionally Christian European world: *agapē*, which was spiritual love, impersonal and meant for every-one equally, and *eros*, also impersonal in the sense that it is largely rooted in biological and instinctual yearning, largely absent of personal, volitional choice. Until that point, love was merely a calcified act of duty: social, political, financial, and legal. Marriage was less an act of love than an act of reinforcing the status quo: "When you think of the Provençal and the Latin word for love, amor, and spell it backward, you get Roma. Rome [the state] was regarded as representing the exact opposite principle to love—and love was held to be the higher principle" (ibid).

Troubadours and the author-poets of the Arthurian romances saw love not as an impersonal, social duty to be per-formed but as a personal revelation, a revelation of the self in service to something higher, something greater. In this way, love reached the level of an ideal, an aesthetic, a calling. No longer could it remain an empty, social convention but instead, as the result of a personal quest, it was understood to be a revelation facilitated by an individual heart. Romantic love was something more too: a dangerous and risky something, a transgression. If marriage was, as Campbell noted, a violation of love, then romantic love must be a violation of the conventions of marriage, a trespassing that surpasses all impediments to the marriage of true minds and true hearts.

In these timeless tales, therefore, love becomes something both familiar and strange, a curse and a revelation. To be truly human means to test limitations even though the cost of doing so may be very high. In *The Romance of Tristan and Iseult*, Iseult's nurse said to Tristan, "In that cup you have drunk not love alone, but love and death together." Understanding that life can never be one thing or the other, Tristan was simple and resolute: "Well then, come Death." Tristan's response conveyed understanding and the acceptance of his actions as well as another, nearly simultaneous, opportunity to transcend limits through death itself! Amfortas, the suffering Grail King, used the cry *"Amor!"* prior to incurring the grievous wound from which he suffered. And in part, he suffered because he was young, callow, and unprepared for the demands, trials, and pain inherent in the revolutionary new force of romantic love. Amfortas imagined *amor* within the conventions of the state, of *Roma*. He may have fared better if he, like Tristan, knew and accepted the dangers of love and had quietly, resolutely uttered the cri de coeur, "Well then, come Death!"

The Rules *of* Enchantment

In this essay, I would like to continue an exploration of the Grail romances and the relevance these stories have to the challenge of living a contemporary life. In Wolfram's *Parzival*, the Grail is described as "a stone vessel brought down from heaven by the neutral angels."

Campbell discusses the symbolic significance of this act in *Romance of the Grail: The Magic and Mystery of Arthurian Myth*. The neutral angels refused to participate in the heavenly war between God and Lucifer, and thus, symbolically, they and their neutrality represent the transcendent function, the aim of which is to reconcile pairs of opposites. Read this way, the Grail and its various narratives are seen not simply as the search for a priceless relic, but rather as an effort to move toward a profoundly life-affirming ideal culminating in healing and wholeness, not just limited to the individual but extending outward to others and to the world itself. It is a union of the spiritual, the psychic, and the physical; it is the phenomenon that C. G. Jung described as the *coniunctio*.

The knights-errant who rode forth seeking the Grail didn't ride under the banner *Amor*, as was the habit of the suffering Grail King, Amfortas. Love is the crooked thing, as W. B. Yeats put it, and there is nobody wise enough to find out all that is in it. One of the things that makes it tricky is that love is often mere convention masquerading as freedom, infatuation posing as deep connection, or an ecstatic projection that leads one unavoidably, at some point, into wounded, impotent grief. Knights-errant striving to attain the Grail labor toward an ideal of chivalry which, contrary to the ecstatic rapture of

Amor, exposes them to difficulties, trials, and suffering—the very experiences that prepare them to apprehend the sublime. Chivalry may well be a generative, procreative quality of the heart, and it gives birth to individual expressions of courage, nobility, mercy, curiosity, patience, and charity. Chivalry expressed as the rules of living lifts the veil on quotidian life to reveal an enchanted world of mystery, of wonder, a world of meaning, a world of soul.

There are people mentioned in the Grail romances who lack the ethos of chivalry, and thus lack what the Grail represents. They live fine, probably even honorable lives as clergy, merchants, farmers, fishmongers, servants, husbands, wives, and children. They, in all likelihood, are not aware that the world in which they work, play, live, feel, speculate, laugh, and finally die is enchanted. All they know of the world is its instinctual pleasures and its unpredictable terrors. For them the world is often harsh, nasty, and short; they commend their souls to God and let fortune do what it must to them, for God and fortune are all they have to rely upon. For them, it's inconceivable to operate in and on the world with anything resembling individual agency because human agency relies upon the qualities of chivalry, and these are qualities that remain unknown to them. Agency knows the value of risk, effort, imagination, and dignity—all those qualities that teach us that breathing is not the same thing as living.

The only chance one has of finding the Grail—or finding what the Grail represents—is through the living of a life predicated on the values of chivalry. Now before you scoff at the notion of chivalry as an antiquated, old-fashioned, straightened notion that contemporary people can disregard, what if I told you that chivalry is not merely a way of life but rather a science? In fact, in his famous paper on phenomenology, "Don Quixote and the Problem of Reality," Alfred Schütz calls chivalry "the queen of all sciences." Chivalry, Schütz argues, encompassed all or most of the known sciences in the world at that time: the knight-errant had to be an expert in criminal and civil law; a theologian; a healer (both physician and herbalist); an economist; an astronomer; an athlete; and an artisan who could shoe a horse, mend a saddle, or repair weapons and armor as the need arose. Above all, the knight-errant had to be a philosopher, one who knew and defended truth while simultaneously understanding that such a defense might well cost him everything, even his own life. In contemporary life, some will see such individuals and identify them as renaissance men, while many others will probably call them fools. But it was said of Don Quixote, and it is no less true of ourselves that one may live as a fool and yet die wise.

The Human Symphony: Notes *from* Asia

As Joseph Campbell notes in *The Masks of God, Volume 2: Oriental Mythology*, there are profoundly different mythologies at work in Eastern and Western cultures, mythologies that create distinctive, and arguably divergent, psychologies in their acolytes, as well as vastly different ways of understanding the natural world and its manifestations, both material and immaterial. And yet, at the same time, one must be cautioned that differences among human beings may often be exaggerated, and that we have more, perhaps much more, in common than we realize. In fact, in Campbell's note on the completion of the *Masks of God* series, he writes:

> Looking back today over the twelve delightful years that I spent on this richly rewarding enterprise, I find that its main result for me has been its confirmation of a thought I have long and faithfully entertained: of the unity of the race of man, not only in its biology but also in its spiritual history, which has everywhere unfolded in the manner of a single symphony, with its themes announced, developed, amplified and turned about, distorted, reasserted and today in a grand fortissimo of all sections sounding together, irresistibly advancing to some kind of mighty climax, out of which the next great movement will emerge.

Additionally, I think that it's fair to note that in the contemporary state of geopolitical and geocultural affairs, many differences between the Western world and Asia are being gradually erased by the process of globalization, which is essentially, it seems to me, a process of corporate capitalism fueled largely by manufacturing and advances in technology. Cultures that were once remote and largely unfamiliar to one another may now, in some respects, share surprising similarities and values. While mindful of the "single symphony" playing in the background, the most striking of the traditional differences between Asia and the West is their differing conceptualizations of ego. In the Western world, and perhaps particularly here in America, emphasis has been placed on developing an individual ego, an individual self, separate and unique from the millions of other egos and selves in the country. The myth of a lone, rugged, resourceful individual, placed at a specific point located in a linear understanding of history, armed with a moral code, a higher truth, or greater skills, and set against the malevolently illiberal, unaware, foolish, or frightened masses, is the story that stirs the American imagination.

In Asia, history is circular rather than linear, and the myth of eternal return is omnipresent in forms that appear and reappear throughout the course of history: the orbits of the sun, the cycles of the moon, the year, and the cycles of life and death. Individual effort cannot fundamentally alter anything; people are not separate from the world, nor are they merely in the vicinity of god, but rather, the task of the individual in traditional Asian culture is to "order his mind as to identify its consciousness with the inhabiting principle of the whole."

Based on the studies he presents in *Oriental Mythology*, Campbell comes to regard what he calls "mythic identification," referred to in this volume and also in *Myths of Light:*

Eastern Metaphors of the Eternal, as among the most important of concepts. The idea is that individuals are not in a relationship to the objects of religious awe, separate and other in the field of time, but instead each individual has the potential to experience that the object of religious or mythic awe is themselves. Each one of us has within ourselves all the gods and demons, all the heavens and hells, all the divine mysteries that fascinate, inspire, and menace. As Campbell beautifully ends this volume, the Eastern effort toward mythic identification and its transcendent realization is "the nectar of the fruit of the tree in the garden that Western man, or at least a notable number of his company, failed to eat."

JOSEPH CAMPBELL:
VIRTUOSO *of the* SUBLIME

In Maurice Doreal's *The Emerald Tablets of Thoth the Atlantean*, there is a saying attributed to Hermes Trismegistus: "As above, so below; as within, so without." This means that whatever happens on any level of reality also happens on every other level, that the individual and the world (indeed, the universe) are holistically linked in the sense that each lies within the other, and by understanding one, we may understand the other. This kind of thinking is metaphorical, but only a metaphorical perspective allows one to soften the adamantine face of materialistic perceptions of reality.

Literalism in the study of myth cannot account for anything remotely like an accurate understanding of the universe and the energies it contains, nor can it accurately account for why human beings experience the world as we do. One may read my indictment of literalness in the study of myth as an indictment of a far more wide-ranging, hegemonic materialism, one that dogmatically pervades contemporary thought, offering the promise of definitive answers topped with certainty, served up in a generous container of self-satisfaction and reductionism, reifying what Erwin Schrödinger called in *My View of the World* the "spatio-temporal plurality of individuals." Schrödinger finished this comment by saying, "but [the spatio-temporal plurality] is a false construction." In his exoteric discussion of scientific thought, Schrödinger asserts that all consciousness is one and simply cannot be spoken of in the plural.

Joseph Campbell turns to Arthur Schopenhauer in *The Inner Reaches of Outer Space* to cite the influence of the same single consciousness to which Schrödinger referred. Campbell likely preferred Schopenhauer for the simple fact that Schopenhauer "had established the prerequisites for a correlation of oriental and occidental metaphysical terms." The dart thrown by Asian mythology landed closest to the center of the great mythological message Campbell most valued, the transcendent experience he called "mythic identification." It is a concept he returns to time and again in his work. Simply stated, the idea of mythic identification is that in which one understands oneself and the objects of religious awe, i.e. the gods, to be one and the same. In mythic identification, one directly identifies with the single consciousness giving rise to the spatio-temporal plurality of things and the accompanying illusion that there are many forms of consciousness.

I'd like to think Campbell would have enjoyed the contemporary philosopher Thomas Nagel and his book *Mind and Cosmos*. In this work, Nagel explores the possibility of imagining a "conception of the natural order very different from materialism—one that makes mind central, rather than a side effect of physical law." In other words, consciousness itself may be the central organizing principle of the universe. As Nagel explains, it is consciousness "rather than physical law, [which] provides the fundamental level of explanation of everything, including the explanation of the basic and universal physical laws themselves."

What I like about Nagel is his willingness to question the logical foundations of accepted facts and beliefs regarding human consciousness. An unquestioning acceptance of materialism is a logical mistake, as is its mirror opposite theism. These poles of thought are severely reductionistic in nature;

they restrict and canalize thinking at the cost of creativity and novelty, insisting that there is only one form and only one way of understanding human existence specifically, and universal existence generally. Here Nagel and Campbell overlap: what Nagel calls reductionism Campbell speaks of as literalization and concretization. When one can let go of reductionisms and forego the easy pleasures of epistemological certainty, one is initiated into a radically reorienting, reordering experience of the sublime.

By my lights, this is what Campbell was all about, the opening of oneself to the sublime, and this move makes Campbell's work perpetually exciting and relevant. Joseph Campbell's work, and in this instance Nagel's as well, reminds me of what Ludwig Wittgenstein wrote in his *Tractatus*: "We feel that even when *all possible* scientific questions have been answered, the problems of life remain completely untouched." The answers to the problems of life lie beyond science and theology, and meanwhile the livable answers await discovery in one's own experience of the sublime. And if Joseph Campbell was a virtuoso of anything, he was truly a virtuoso of the sublime.

WHAT WILL BE, IS

In his 1944 preface to *A Skeleton Key to "Finnegans Wake,"* Joseph Campbell calls Joyce's book "a kind of terminal moraine in which lie buried all the myths, programs, slogans, hopes, prayers, tools, educational theories, and theological bric-a-brac of the past millennium." It's apropos, then, that Joyce's main character in *Finnegans Wake* is named Humphrey Chimpden Earwicker, HCE, or as Joyce refers to him, **H**ere **C**omes **E**veryone. HCE is, himself, a terminal moraine in human form. When *Finnegans Wake* was published in 1939— you can see what an early enthusiast Campbell was—many critics didn't know what to make of it. Vladimir Nabokov, for instance, thought *Ulysses* to be the finest book of the twentieth century, but found *Finnegans Wake* to be "formless and dull," "a tragic failure," and "a frightful bore." After all these years, I can't decide if I think Nabokov may have been wrong in his assessment of *Finnegans Wake*, though I am absolutely sure he was right in his admiration for *Ulysses*. In *Finnegans Wake*, it seems as though Joyce abandoned any regard at all for his readers. It's hard to find any narrative traction, and while *Finnegans Wake* may be wrought from the English language, it is certainly not written in English, but rather in some strange "Nichtian glossery which purveys aprioric roots for aposteriorious tongues"; as Joyce writes, "this is nat language in any sinse of the world" (*Finnegans Wake*, 83).

But Campbell found traction in *Finnegans Wake*, and boy did he ever: "Underneath the verbal ambiguities and philologic traps of the Wake, deep speaks to deep about such everyday matters as marital discord, sibling strife, military slaughter, racial violence, theological differences and financial thimblerigging—fascinating material that academicians (at their peril) fail to discuss or continue to ignore."What's more, Campbell sensed the profound influence that the work of Friedrich Nietzsche exerted upon Joyce: "Nietzsche's description of his own creative struggle, 'I write in blood, I will be read in blood,' is applicable tenfold to Joyce." But I'll return to that "Nichtian" influence in a moment.

Perhaps it may seem odd, then, that the only thing approaching a ritual that I've associated with the arrival of the new year in the past two decades or so is reading from *Finnegans Wake*.

At some point, near the end of December or the beginning of January, I read the last lines of *Finnegans Wake* and let their beautiful rhythm carry me serenely along, as though drifting down the Liffey itself, "So soft this morning, ours" and a bit later, "End here. Us then. Finn, again!" And finally, Joyce tells me I hold the key to the whole thing: "A way a lone a last a loved a long the" . . . and thus endeth *Finnegans Wake*. But in this book, as it almost certainly is in life, the end is not really the end. This is the key to life that Joyce offers his readers. That last sentence of the book is really the first part of the sentence that begins the novel: "riverrun, past Eve and Adam's, from swerve of shore to bend of bay, brings us by a commodious vicus of recirculation back to Howth Castle and Environs." Joyce is describing the nature of mythic time: circular, recurring, nonlinear. There are no beginnings or endings, only the eternally recurring flow.

Circling back to Nietzsche's influence on Joyce, we arrive at the notion of eternal recurrence, an idea central to Nietzsche's philosophy. Eternal recurrence is Nietzsche's theory that suggests that since time is infinite, the things in the flow of time are finite (atoms and events, your life and all your experiences), and these finite events, such as your life exactly as you have lived it, will recur again and again and again innumerable times. As Nietzsche remarked in *The Gay Science*, how well disposed to oneself and one's life one would have to be in order to crave nothing more than this, and still be able to say, "and never have I heard anything more divine!" This is the epitome of radical self-acceptance, not merely bearing the circumstances of one's life because there is no other choice but rather to be determined to love it all. That's the move Nietzsche called *Amor Fati*, the love of one's own fate, and it may be the most burdensome, and at the same time the most awesome of our responsibilities to ourselves.

Saying—no, shouting—yes to life is the affirming declaration of and for life. The eternal yes is not a call to reformation or redemption, but rather a welcoming acceptance of life exactly as it is, embracing the creative, sustaining, destructive nature of life itself. It's Molly Bloom's *Yes!* at the end of *Ulysses*, and like Molly, Anna Livia Plurabelle is in *Finnegans Wake* "the carrier of the Eternal Yes; . . . Men, cities, empires, and whole systems bubble and burst in her river of time" (*Skeleton Key*, 362). As it is with dreams, the more we live with them, reflect upon them, marvel at the symbols and puzzles they bring us, the more meaningful they are to us. And so it is with Joyce's dream of a book *Finnegans Wake*. And, as I find with most symbolic puzzles, Campbell stands nearby, enthusiastically pointing the way.

A Mind *of* Myth

We all know things. In fact, we all know a lot of things about a lot of things. The human brain is stunningly complex: a newborn baby has somewhere around 100 billion neurons, twice as many as adults, and in a brain half the size. No wonder a child's brain from birth to around the age of three functions as a knowledge sponge, constantly learning new things, all sorts of things. The extravagant diversity of thingness makes the world and its inhabitants an utter wonder. Most of us grow up learning to have a mind of things, filled with the qualities of things and the heuristic schemas that help us manipulate those things. Materialism constitutes the foundation of most human learning. For example, parents speak to children materially: What animal is this? What color is that? How many fingers do you have? We ask children to perform counting, but we seldom go beyond material applications and ask them, for example, what numbers actually are. We never ask them whether ourselves or our universe is real, whether there's free will, or an objective reality. We never ask them why there is something instead of nothing. It's proper, of course, that we don't introduce metaphysics and existentialism to young children, for they would likely dissolve into an angsty goo right before our inquisitive eyes, and parents would be forced to save for their child's long-term psychoanalysis rather than college.

In *Thou Art That*, Joseph Campbell notes that Zen masters always dissolve the material world by including the opposite immediately after whatever object or concept they might reference: "That which is no thing. That which is not that. This is the ultimate reference of our metaphors . . . opening the mystery of the operation of this transcendent energy in the field of time and space." And in *Myths of Light*, Campbell writes, "You cannot say a thing either is or is not. The things are no things, there is nothing there. Here, below, all things [are] dual. This line is the mystery of *māyā*. The word *māyā* comes from a root *ma*, which means 'to measure forth; to build.' *Māyā* is what builds forth the world." It's easy to imagine Lear's Fool as a Hindu scholar when he asks King Lear, "Can you make no use of nothing, nuncle?"

Myth's foundation is metaphor, and metaphors are the no-things of which myth makes the most extraordinary use; correspondingly, a mind of myth makes use of everything. Living often gets in the way of understanding life and seeing through the illusions of materiality, but a mind of myth saves one from the emptiness of a life lived solely, and soullessly, on its surface. A mind of myth frees one from the pernicious distraction of pursuing happiness. Furthermore, myth saves us from a too-remote, too-sterile history, one that neglected to send a salubrious message in a bottle downstream to those of us in the present who struggle to find meaning in a history largely content to present the past as a quaint curiosity.

Developing a mind of myth requires one to think mythically, striving to see through the world of appearance, the world of convention, the world of belief, to even see through life and death. Our challenge is to see through the literalized world to a world in which nothing is not a contradiction of terms. In his poem "The Snow Man," Wallace Stevens wrote:

> One must have a mind of winter
> To regard the frost and the boughs

Of the pine-trees crusted with snow;
And have been cold a long time
To behold the junipers shagged with ice,
The spruces rough in the distant glitter
Of the January sun; and not to think
Of any misery in the sound of the wind,
In the sound of a few leaves,
Which is the sound of the land
Full of the same wind
That is blowing in the same bare place
For the listener, who listens in the snow,
And, nothing himself, beholds
Nothing that is not there and the nothing that is.

A mind of myth is created from a long, uncompromising practice of saying yes to the world exactly as it is, yes to all its suffering and pain, its joy, its beauty, its impenetrability, its staggering disregard for human concern. A mind of myth is the result of saying yes to "the full catastrophe," as Zorba put it, and heeding the call to the symbolic life that is itself the mysterious *māyā* that gives rise to human consciousness and existence. It isn't simply knowing the stories of mythology that help one develop a mind of myth; one must inhabit them until thinking mythologically becomes second nature, until one is able to see the nothing that is not there and the no-thing that is. The ability to do just that was Joseph Campbell's particular genius.

THE MYSTERIES *at* ELEUSIS:
DIFFERENT *and* LUCKIER

My grandfather was a farmer in rural Minnesota on land that was homesteaded by my great-grandfather in the late nineteenth century. It was a small farm by today's standards, not much more than eighty acres or so. I remember childhood Augusts spent wandering around in the fields, along creeks, or through a grove of apple trees. Time on the farm in August moved slowly, languidly, while crops like wheat and corn relaxed into an eye-pleasingly warm, golden color; fruits and berries hung pendulously off branches and vines; grasses were cool, thick, and luxurious, and even the August air had a voluptuous, distended quality that made life itself seem idly rich, a little insouciant, and blithely serene.

Those memories often lead me to wonder what agrarian life was like several thousand years ago, what it taught us about life and death, about seasonal patience, hard work, and being at the mercy of the elements. Perhaps to a surprising degree, these concerns, especially those of life and death, were assuaged by ritual initiations into received teachings of mystery cults like the Mystery Cult at the Sanctuary of Eleusis, a religion established around Demeter and Persephone, which endured for nearly two thousand years and attracted initiates from all over the civilized world (see Carl Kerényi's *Eleusis: Archetypal Image of Mother and Daughter*).

Joseph Campbell points out in *Goddesses: Mysteries of the Divine Feminine* that, unlike summer on my grandfather's farm in the North American Midwest, "In the Greek summer, fierce heat dries up the vegetation, so during the summer the grain that was harvested in the spring was stored in silos in the ground. Hence the wealth of the culture is in and under the ground, in the domain of Hades." Because all the images and symbols in it refer to agricultural technology, the Demeter and Persephone myth makes a great deal more sense when one keeps in mind that times of planting and harvest are reversed in the more northern latitudes from those of the Mediterranean world.

It's also important to note that Hades, or Plutus, is not only the god of the underworld; he's also the god of wealth, not just the cultural wealth Campbell mentioned but also the mineral wealth found beneath the earth's surface. In a sense, the mineral wealth and siloed grain fills the earth in the same way a cornucopia is abundantly filled, its contents often overflowing. The cornucopia is an important symbol in the Eleusinian Mysteries and represents the wealth residing in one's own unconscious psychic potential and the abundant gifts discernable in the midst of living one's life, if only one knows how to look and how to see.

The entire purpose of the mystery rites at Eleusis was for the initiate to be introduced into a way of seeing that apprehends a profoundly rapturous, overwhelming vision similar to what theologians in the Middle Ages called the *visio beatifica*. The *visio* was the beholding of God, a direct revelation of God from God to the viewer who, once having seen it, achieved eternal blessedness. The Eleusinian Mysteries also culminated in a seeing, the difference being that while the *visio beatifica* was revelatory, it was still relational; there still remained distance between the seer and the seen, whereas in the Eleusinian rites the seer achieved *epopteia*, an ability to see the inner god shining through the human being, to see, in all senses of the word, that one has become One with divinity, that life isn't extinguished by death, that death is, ultimately, nothing to fear. In Kundalini yoga, this is the realization at the opening of the seventh and final chakra. *Epopteia* is consistent with Campbell's concept of mythic identification in which one realizes that one is oneself the object of religious awe.

It's hard to say exactly what happened at Eleusis, partly because speaking about the ritual was, as Campbell puts it, "a mortal offense." The rituals were a secret "kept by hundreds of thousands of people (*Goddesses*, 192)." We are given clues to some aspects of the ritual based on drawings and carvings on kraters and sarcophagi, from the fact that Aeschylus was put on trial and eventually acquitted for violating the omertà around the rituals, and that the notoriously narcissistic, treasonous sot Alcibiades is said to have staged scenes from the rites in his home. Later, the Apostolic Fathers, while writing to discredit the Mysteries, described aspects of the rites associated with them. The end of the Mysteries came around 400 CE when Alaric, King of the Goths, accompanied by his soldiers and black-robed monks, poured through the Pass of Thermopylae and overran Greece.

What we do know from *Eleusis: Archetypal Image of Mother and Daughter* is that "the initiate possessed a knowledge which conferred blessedness, and not only in the hereafter; both knowledge and beatitude became his possession the moment he beheld the vision." This epiphany was repeated again and again, year after year, over a period of nearly two thousand years. Invariably, the initiate was filled with knowledge, blessedness, beauty, and bliss. It was such a satisfying physical and spiritual fullness that it lasted, according to a profusion of accounts, one's whole life long. Walt Whitman probably never heard of the Eleusinian Mysteries, but he sums them up perfectly in his great poem "Song of Myself":

> The smallest sprout shows there is really no death;
> And if ever there was it led forward life, and does not
> wait at the end to arrest it,
> And ceas'd the moment life appear'd.
>
> All goes onward and outward, nothing collapses,
> And to die is different from what any one supposed,
> and luckier.

THE PROVINCE *of the* PRIMITIVE

In Joseph Campbell's *The Masks of God, Volume 1: Primitive Mythology*, he writes, "We shall be finding clues to the deepest secrets not only of the high cultures of both the Orient and the Occident, but also of our own most inward expectations, spontaneous responses, and obsessive fears."

Our own most inward expectations, spontaneous responses and obsessive fears have not markedly changed since the dawn of human history; modern *Homo sapiens* does not think or imagine much differently than its prehistoric ancestors. In fact, the same rational, imaginative abilities invented the atlatl as well as the laptop, and the art of cave painters remains, in the opinion of many, even Picasso, unsurpassed in any subsequent era. In his delightful, often astonishing book *Out of Our Minds: What We Think and How We Came to Think It*, Felipe Fernández-Armesto writes,

> Over the entire history of our species, no evidence of any overall change is discernible, for better or worse, in the skill with which humans think. Maybe there was an era, long before the emergence of Homo Sapiens, when life was 'poor, nasty, brutish and short' and hominids scavenged without leisure for ratiocination; but for hundreds of thousands of years thereafter all our ancestors, as far as we know, were relatively leisured foragers rather than relatively harried, hasty scavengers.

The phrase "harried, hasty scavengers" seems to describe very well what many of us in contemporary life have become. People work more jobs and more hours and have more stress, fewer resources, longer lives, and worse health. A life of relative leisure sounds pretty good in comparison, and it turns out that in some important ways modern humans may be more "primitive" than our prehistoric ancestors were. Which brings us to that problematic word *primitive*. Primitive conjures many associations: nontechnological, illiterate, small, uncivilized, and isolated. If one is honest, there can hardly be an argument that for most, the word *primitive* is synonymous with inferior, that primitive or savage (another unfortunate word) people are akin to superstitious children, ignorant to the nature or structure of the world, of morality, indeed, of life itself.

The original copyright date of *Primitive Mythology* was 1959, a time when the use of the word *primitive* was common in scholarly papers, textbooks, and as general linguistic currency. But reading this volume of Campbell's work, I find that the pejorative sense of the word is lacking. Instead, one finds in Campbell's writing a persistent sense of wonder and awe attending the unremitting human project. My reading of Campbell is that he finds no mind literally primitive, but rather sees "more sophisticated . . . visions of the local traditions, wherein those mythologies themselves will be known to be but the masks of a larger . . . 'timeless schema' that is no schema." For humans, ideas and images make the world, and they have much more force and effect than impersonal forces or the material exigencies of life. Human imagination and thought respond to life's circumstance and reimagine the world in a way we then literally try to create. The evolution of culture is grounded in the fundamental idea that individuals change, that they take on qualities that did not ancestrally or congenitally belong to them. They become different from what they once were, and together these individuals may create a world that does not yet exist. Humanity's greatest hope lies in the human imagination.

Imagination is not inspired by myths. Rather, myths are products of imagination. Human imagination has the capacity to imagine things that aren't and things that are in a different way. The power of the human imagination armed with myth has the power to dive deep into the hidden world and explore the forces and energies that inform the material world. In *Primitive Mythology*, I think that Campbell himself saw through the dismissive trope of primitivism of the late 1950s and wanted:

> to make it serve the present hour, . . . to assemble—or reassemble—it in its full dimension, scientifically, and then bring it to life as our own, in the way of art: the way of wonder—sympathetic, instructive delight; not judging morally, but participating with our own awakened humanity in the festival of the passing forms."

The mythic images and passing forms are themselves, as Campbell often noted, essentially poetic, and like all poetry they are employed in a dialogue with all we know, all we think we know, all we don't know, and all we're afraid to know. I think myth begins in, and should always remain informed by, skepticism. Myths arise because of doubts about the nature of reality and curiosity about that which we cannot quite apprehend. Entertaining doubt moves one closer to the light, closer to truth; skepticism is the hallmark of the arts and sciences, the interdependent domains that make possible the flowering of both individuals and civilizations.

THE UNDISCOVERED COUNTRY

Let's take a moment to examine death—as Hamlet put it, "the undiscover'd country from whose bourn no traveler returns." Death is the most enduring, and probably the most dreadful problem to face animals of the genus *Homo*. In *The Masks of God, Volume 1:Primitive Mythology*, Campbell writes that the "human being is the only animal capable of knowing death as the end inevitable for itself, and the span of old age for this human organism, consciously facing death, is a period of years longer than the whole lifetime of any other primate." Facing death is complicated by circumstances such as ineradicable comas and persistent vegetative states, the final stages of chronic, debilitating diseases that remove the sufferer's ability to communicate, and other diabolical conditions that make it difficult to determine the difference between life and death.

Early peoples began speculating about what death might be based on the experiences they had in life, particularly the nature of the life they observed in the world around them. As Campbell noted, "Among the hunting tribes, whose lifestyle is based on the art of killing, who live in a world of animals that kill and are killed and hardly know the organic experience of a natural death, all death is a consequence of violence and is generally ascribed not to the natural destiny of temporal beings but to magic."

Magic, he says, became the technology employed, not only to defend oneself against death but to deliver death to others as well. Understood this way, death is an enemy to be fought off, held at bay, and resisted to the bitter end. *"For the planting folk,"* however, "death is a natural phase of life, comparable to the moment of the planting of the seed, for rebirth" (ibid., 107). Through an agrarian lens, life and death are naturally cyclical, and there was, just beyond physical life and death, a larger ground of being of which one had only hunches or intuitions. And with the slightest effort of imagination, one easily finds similarities in the image of a farmer harvesting wheat with a sickle to the shrouded, skeletal image of the Grim Reaper, scythe in hand, similarly severing souls from bodies. These various intuitions and images eventually coalesce, and somewhere around the second millennium BCE the notion of immortality is refined, and ideas like eternal rewards or punishments begin to make death arguably the most important part of life.

Four thousand years on, one may reasonably insist that we haven't added significantly to our understanding of death. The people of that distant age seem instantly recognizable to ourselves in that, like them, we still wrestle with the mystery of death, we have the same hopes and fears about life, and the same challenges of human nature. Near-death experiences and visions described by the dying tell us nothing about death as those events speak only to dying, which then necessarily leads one to consider that the important death, the death for which biological death serves as a metaphor, is psychological death.

Psychological death, sometimes referred to as the death of the ego, provokes a profound, and a profoundly difficult, transformation of the psyche. All the familiar, comforting ways in which one routinely thinks about and understands oneself drop away—one's purpose, identity, rationality, moral fiber, character—and one is left apparently empty, a self that is a stranger to itself. Coming to consciousness is seldom a serene act; it's usually terrifying and often accompanied by violence, or at least intimations or threats of violence, and disorientation. One undergoes a form of psychic decline in which trusted inner constructs crumble and logical relationships to thoughts and experiences dissolve.

Of course, it makes sense that it should be so; no one makes radical changes when life is comfortable. The psychological death prepares the psychic ground for rebirth and greater growth; it makes untenable the merely fantastical and performative postures of goodness, success, knowledge, and happiness, and one is forced to confront the totality of oneself. It's not likely that one is ever completely good, or perfectly happy, and that deep down what we think of as success is often nothing more than a comforting illusion. Any number of harsh truths that are in some way unique to one's own experience of living, and to the community in which one lives, will be revealed.

As Stanton Marlan wrote in *The Black Sun: The Alchemy and Art of Darkness*, "Death fertilizes the imaginal and works to open a poetic space that brings depth and meaning to everyday life." Indeed, death insists upon a deeper, more richly nuanced connection to one's own unconscious, the unfolding of our own lives, and that of existence itself. The psychological death gives rise to patience, humility, empathy, and ultimately transcendence of the old self. It is such a radical reconfiguration of the self that one may even become excited by the thought of it and say, "But I will be a bridegroom in my death, and run into 't as a lover's bed" (Shakespeare, *Antony and Cleopatra*, Act IV).

SCARES *and* SCARS

Scars are curious things given an even more curious name: the word *scar* is derived from the Greek word *eschara*, meaning "place of fire." The word does not mean "caused by fire," nor does it mean that scars are the result of exposing one's skin to fire, although there is a connection to the Latin word for scab. No, *scar* means quite literally, the place of fire: the fire is found within the scar, and the scar is already present in the fire. Perhaps its derivation has to do with the sensation of intense, searing pain, the kind of pain borne by the body at the receipt of a wound, a wound on fire with pain and deep enough to create scarring.

The most familiar English usage defines a scar as a mark left on the skin after a surface injury or wound has healed. Scars commemorate and memorialize. They freeze time, space, and emotion in pale, sometimes jagged and awkwardly etched lines on the skin, and not infrequently, they leave a jagged signature upon the heart as well. And even though there is no apparent etymological relationship between them, one can't resist adding an *e* to scar to create the word *scare*. A scary encounter leaves scars; even children know that. Intense fear—being scared to death, for instance—leaves its deeply etched mark upon the mind even though the frightening event has long since passed. In fact, it is often the scar no one else can see that is the hardest to bear.

Scars also serve as a means of identification: if one ever has the misfortune of being booked into jail, one of the questions that will be asked of you is whether you have any birthmarks, tattoos, or scars. Scars are an ancient way of confirming one's identity. One of the most poignant accounts of recognition and identification may be found in Book XIX of the *Odyssey*, when the disguised Odysseus (transfigured to look like an old, decrepit beggar by Athena) is given a bath by his old nurse-maid, Eurycleia. As she begins to bathe him, she recognizes the scar on his thigh, received as a small boy when he was gored by a boar, and through her recognition of the scar identifies Odysseus. Her eyes fill with tears, a mixture of grief and joy, as she clutches him by his beard and calls him her dear boy. For he who was thought to be dead is alive again, and Odysseus, himself lost, is found.

For the lover longing for the beloved, the scar is a welcome affirmation of the beloved's presence. The scar is an insepa-rable part of the beloved herself, and any thought of it ipso facto incarnates the beloved; so much so, in fact, that the scar may become as much an object of love as the loved one herself. Writing of Christ's scars in his book *City of God*, St. Augustine expresses a similar sentiment when he says that they (Christ's scars) will not "be a deformity, but [have] a dignity in them; and a certain kind of beauty will shine in them, in the body, though not of the body."

This is an essential idea to take note of, and it bears repeat-ing that the body does not manufacture the beauty shining in and through the scars, as it is a most imperfect vessel. If the body does not produce beauty, then what does? Beauty is, in fact, created by a powerful alchemy involving a scarring wound, a loving gaze, and a precious foundling, all culminating in a moment of poetry and illumination, a moment in which love is transformed from an abstract, vaguely meaningful word into a living, breathing, human disclosure that declares that the wound is the essence of the beloved and must be equally loved for its power of revelation.

The scar and its shadow are made deeper and darker by attempts to recoil and hide from them, and one's anguish is compounded because the attempts to conceal one's scars inevitably fail, until finally one wears one's scars as a symbol of everything corrupt, debauched, perverted, and subverted within. Nothing emanating from such an internal state can be anything but grotesquely and tragically flawed. For that reason, witches, demons, trolls and monsters are frequently described as having ugly, terrifying scars.

Whenever two previously unrelated things are joined together, a scar (or a seam if you will) is always the result, and when individuals are joined to previously unknown and unconscious aspects of themselves, some psychic scarring is the painful and inescapable consequence. It can only be ever thus: only when one is faced with something overwhelming can the archetype of wholeness be constellated. So do not be ashamed of scars. Valorize them; caress them; trace their course on your skin and in your mind's eye. Scars are roadways drawn onto maps of flesh, leading always to the beautiful truths buried deep within oneself.

THE BIRTH *of* TENDERNESS

Gratitude is an interesting assortment of feelings, a complex emotion that I think leads one to experience what was one of Friedrich Hölderlin's favorite words, *zärtlichkeit*, which translates in English to "tenderness." When I feel gratitude, I also notice that I feel peaceful, warmhearted, generous, gentle, humane, and kindly disposed to the world and those in it; I feel what Hannah Arendt called "a palpating tenderness toward the things of the world."

The attitude and emotion of tenderness is a difficult thing to achieve, mostly because a "palpating tenderness" is most reliably awakened while participating in (as Joseph Campbell put it) the sorrows of the world, among the most poignant of which is the realization that any material, literal, complete understanding of life exists just beyond one's grasp.

Joseph Campbell gives us an example of a beautifully tender moment in a tale found in his edition of *The Thousand and One Nights*. A character in one of the stories, Bedreddin, is rebuffed by his son Agib, for whom he feels an uncanny love (both of them happen to be unaware they're related): "In thy bright visage is a sign that may not be fulfilled, And there all beauties that incite to tenderness are shown. Must I then die of thirst, while thy lips with nectar flow? Thy face is Paradise to me; must I in hell-fire groan?" Agib's refusal is a dicey moment for Bedreddin in that he simply cannot understand his feelings for this beautiful young man, yet he is compelled to willingly risk his own life should he offend Agib with his intense attention. Bedreddin was inhabiting what Hölderlin would have called "*im zarten Augenblicke*," the tender moment. Acting against one's own self-interested instincts seems to be an important factor in the realization of tenderness.

Speaking of instincts, *zärtlichkeit* is a word often found in the collected works of Sigmund Freud. In Freud's psychoanalytic writing, tenderness is at times presented as problematic, but in the final analysis, Freud concludes that tenderness is awakened when the sexual instinct is sublimated. One cannot help, I think, sensing a larger truth at work, operating in such a way to insist that sexuality is merely a single thread in the totality of the psyche (C. G. Jung certainly thought so). It may well be that the successful transformation of any self-interested, instinctual impulse or desire into generosity and benevolence is the gateway to gratitude and, finally, tenderness. One can't help but be tenderly inclined to others as well as the world if one is grateful for existence, grateful for the experience of accepting and living life on life's own terms. I believe that is the sentiment behind many of Freud's therapeutic intentions and I, at least, find a great deal of tenderness living in his well-known comment that the aim of psychoanalysis is to transform neurotic suffering into common unhappiness.

I'm always impressed with how tough and tough-minded Freud had to be in order to make us all aware of how we move through life pretending (and often unaware that we're pretending) to ourselves and others to be something we are not. He cast a light on the substantial darkness and inner conflicts arising from instincts and desires within each one of us, showed us that our most cherished notions, our highest ideals, were not entirely free from uncharitable selfishness or other base motives. Moreover, one's inner darkness reaches out to tenderness and, in doing so, connects one to a rather puzzling, nonrational sense of wonder and Plutonic richness. In my gratitude for Freud's trailblazing, strenuous effort, I find, not surprisingly, a deep tenderness for the old lion.

To achieve gratitude and tenderness one must act with intention; both require a self-aware choice, and that choice is, more often than not, preceded by a struggle within oneself between the atavistic, self-serving motives and the heartful, noble motives. But the struggle itself creates an opportunity to summon gratitude and tenderness—not least of all, for ourselves—the territory that, by all indications, Joseph Campbell inhabited quite naturally.

Perhaps because Campbell came spontaneously, eagerly, and unpretentiously to self-direction and self-discipline, he was congenitally inclined to attitudes of wonder and awe, particularly in his encounters with the natural world. Astonishingly, according to *Joseph Campbell: A Fire in the Mind: The Authorized Biography,* he was developing in his late twenties concepts he would continue to refine over the course of his life:

> an amalgam of Joyce's 'aesthetic arrest' and Campbell's own unique distillate which he would cite in print some twenty years later as his "first function of any living mythology": to awaken a sense of awe and wonder in response to the unfathomable mystery of the universe.

I think it was Campbell's remarkable capacity for awe which allowed him to, in large part, choose to move through life with an attitude of conscious gratitude and a compassionate tenderness that soothed the sorrows of living.

THE STILL POINT *of the* TURNING WORLD

At the still point of the turning world.
Neither flesh nor fleshless;
Neither from nor towards; at the still point,
there the dance is . . .
—T.S. Eliot, "Burnt Norton"

It is often the case that in the final months of the year we have a sense of the present turning into the future, of dark turning to light, of aging. To deepen one's understanding of and connection to life, one must turn from the literal, inexorable passage of time to the inner enterprise of finding "the still point of the turning world." That phrase, the still point of the turning world, written by T.S. Eliot, was one that Joseph Campbell often quoted while describing a state of release from the delusions, fears, and commitments "by which lives in this world are compelled to their sorrows and pains." (*The Inner Reaches of Outer Space: Metaphor as Myth and as Religion*, p.106) A state of release or illumination is achieved by learning to see through the illusions the effort of living compels us to create, learning to see through the numberless obscuring images, beliefs, and ideas we collect, and apprehend the dynamics of the soul itself. "The required method to this end," Campbell teaches, "is known as the turning about of the energy," a shift in which we bring all our energies to bear on these qualities as they exist within ourselves, and "not outward to the correction of the world" (p. 38).

Such a mechanism for seeing through the ephemera of existence exists innately; it is an archetypal movement belonging to the soul that I have called "leave-taking." All things flow, Heraclitus noticed, and nothing remains the same or holds its shape forever. The leavings and the losses, the growing and the groaning, the knowings and the no-ings, altered states of consciousness, birth, death, and change—change, change, change—seem all too often to constitute the greater part of living. I call this movement leave-taking because the soul is always and invariably drawing one away from a place of familiarity, of physical and emotional comfort, and plunging one into situations of confusion, risk, and psychic danger. The soul urges one to leave the known and the familiar for the unknown and undreamt of.

We are, on this spinning world, constantly in the situation of turning: turning toward, turning away, turning in, turning out, turning around, and even turning upside down. The poet, Rainer Maria Rilke puts it this way:

> Who has turned us around like this, so that whatever
> we do, we find ourselves in the attitude of someone
> going away? Just as that person on the last hill, which
> shows him his whole valley one last time, turns, stops,
> lingers—so we live forever taking our leave ("Eighth
> Duino Elegy," *The Essential Rilke*, 129).

Plato writes in *Timaeus* that within the soul was formed the "corporeal universe, and brought the two together and united them center to center. The soul, interfused everywhere from the center to the circumference of heaven, of which also she is the external envelopment, herself turning in herself.." Plato's answer to Rilke is that it's the soul that turns us around (and inside out) and bids us say our goodbyes.

Leave-taking, at first blush, always seems like a loss; it's a kind of dying, and it's a death that's generally attended by suffering and fear. We often seek to avoid suffering and try to recreate a safe, secure, womb-like existence at the cost, of course, of our own stillborn life. It is as if we are only able to know something as we lose it, as we let go, as we witness its decay and decline. It is as if leave-taking supplies us with the knowledge of what something is in itself. It is in its absence that we find the meaning and importance of what we once beheld.

It's often the case that the separations, losses, and turnings of life are regarded as obstacles to living and misfortunes to be avoided or, if possible, mastered by individual expressions of will. But I think that the archetypal leave-taking movement of the soul is in no small way the soul's quintessence. Leave-taking is an encompassing psychic reality separate from ego directed activities. If that distinction is not made, one impulsively, unironically, and unconsciously undertakes a series of geographic relocations, or ends relationships and quits jobs, all in the desperate hope that Psyche's relentless call to conscious awareness of the soul's archetypal movement can be quieted.

While I believe that one may not experience the soul's leave-taking movement without a sense of grief or loss, the grief and loss needn't be understood as a tragic, ultimately doomed struggle against life. Seen as an expression of the soul, the leave-takings we're subjected to may even make us more tenderly disposed to life. The paradoxical psychic tensions generated between safety and loss are essential to living and are constituents of the very tensions that sustain life itself. Paradox is the lure that fuels an obsession with the evanescent, shimmering mystery of existence, and as it vanishes and reappears, it draws one along after. And since leaving is fundamental to living, we should take a cue from Shakespeare's *Macbeth*, and not be shy about embracing it: "And let us not be daintie of leave-taking, but shift away."

THE ANCIENT CRAFT *of the* BEAUTIFUL

Reading the exploration of mythology and dance in Joseph Campbell's book *The Ecstasy of Being: Mythology and Dance*, I am reminded that mythology itself was once thought of as a primary subject, what Burton Feldman and Robert D. Richardson Jr. called in *The Rise of Modern Mythology, 1680–1860* "a master field of the first importance." The study of myth was undertaken because it was believed to be a key to the proper understanding of not only religion but of language, history, philosophy, and art, including dance. Identifying mythology as a master discipline is to differ from contemporary assumptions about myth that inevitably place it within the subset of other disciplines. Nevertheless, the power of myth is still robust; myth is read into just about any subject as a way to support or discredit arguments. This plasticity of myth, coupled with its ubiquity, creates a peculiar sort of double vision that understands the fact that myth exists, and that it has more than a little to say about the human psyche that creates such extraordinary and unusual ideas.

The ubiquity, plasticity, and power of myth are rooted in its use of metaphor. Hannah Arendt wrote that "since Homer the metaphor has borne that element of the poetic which conveys cognition; its use establishes the correspondences between physically most remote things. . . . Metaphors are the means by which the oneness of the world is poetically brought about." In *The Ecstasy of Being*, Campbell spends some time discussing Isadora Duncan and emphasizes her revelation regarding the way in which the Parthenon reflects fundamental ideas of nature itself: "Not in imitation of the outside forms of nature, but in understanding of nature's great, secret rules." Metaphor, meaning "to transfer," enables us, Arendt says, to give material form to the invisible and thus to render it capable of being experienced. This experience of the invisible is a fine way to define ecstasy. Similarly, the philosopher to whom I am most affectionately disposed, Emil Cioran, wrote in *The New Gods* that ecstasy's "object is a god without attributes, an essence of god," and somehow Isadora managed to spend surprisingly large portions of her life in such a state.

In the March 1, 1936, issue of *Esquire* magazine, nine years after her death, John Dos Passos published what has become one of my most enduringly favorite essays, called "Art and Isadora," in which he captures the "divine dancer as a figure of earth leading a flight from materialism in a flutter of Greek robes and unpaid bills." Consciously or not, Dos Passos, in describing Isadora as a figure of earth, affirms her insistence that great art is not an imitation of nature, but is itself *Natura* expressing in a material form. At some level Dos Passos understood this and remarked, "Art was whatever Isadora did."

In Athens Isadora stood, day after day, awe-struck before the Parthenon and

> as I stood there my body was as nothing and my soul was scattered; but gradually called by the great inner voice of the Temple, came back the parts of myself to worship it . . . and I did not dare move, for I realized that of all the movements my body had made none was worthy to be mad before a Doric Temple. And as I stood thus I realized that I must find a dance whose effort was to be worthy of this Temple—or never dance again (*The Ecstasy of Being*, p. 110).

When the daimon seizes one in this manner, one has no choice but to surrender to it or become deadened to life—one's own *and* the life of the collective. The deadening consists of an emotional and mental demise that consigns one to the vestibule of hell alongside those others who refused to commit to something more than themselves.

But simply committing or surrendering to one's daimon doesn't ensure happiness or security either, and certainly Isadora was such an example. She and her family were often broke, and Dos Passos notes, "They were never more than one jump ahead of the sheriff, they were always wheedling the tradespeople out of bills, jumping the rent, getting handouts from rich Philistines for art." Isadora drank too much, she didn't even try to control her sexual appetites, her relationships generally imploded, and she had more than her share of tragedy and loss. But the beatings we receive from life are often a part of the price we pay for bliss, and no matter how hard she fell she remained, as Campbell put it, "a living image of enraptured spontaneity, Greek in its inspiration, earthly and physical in its beauty."

Art was indeed whatever Isadora did, including dying. At the age of fifty she found a handsome, and of course young, mechanic with a sporty car, and when one day he drove up to carry her away, she got in, artfully threw her long scarf around her neck, and bid her friends goodbye saying, *"Adieu mes amis je vais à la glorie!"* (Farewell my friends, I go to glory!) They sped away, and Dos Passos describes Isadora's "heavy trailing scarf caught in a wheel, wound tight. Her head was wrenched against the side of the car. The car stopped instantly, her neck was broken, her nose crushed, Isadora was dead."

Merci d'avoir lu ceci.

FORSAKING *the* EASY
for the HARDER PLEASURES

Artists—and I mean to include not just visual artists but writers, dancers, musicians, actors, and others, even intellectuals, who bring subtlety and passion to their pursuits, those that draw their work from the contemplation of the *mysterium tremendum*, the great mystery of existence—have always had a monumental impact on culture. To a person, they unflinchingly blazed new trails in their chosen realms; they were passionately committed to their visions, determined to follow the inner call of their daemons, oblivious to the judgments of the wider world. They are examples of people bold enough to entertain ecstasy and courageous enough to follow their bliss.

The English word *ecstasy* is derived from the Greek word *ekstasis*, which literally means to be standing outside of oneself, carried beyond individual, rational thought to a psychosomatic state in which rationality and personal volition are suspended. It creates a transcendent state, an experience of the world—the universe, even—as unified, timeless, unbounded, and harmonious. This is, I think, close to what Campbell called bliss.

But the word *bliss* has some etymological baggage, descending as it does from Old English and Old Saxon words with meanings like merriment, happiness, grace, and gentleness. These kinds of innocent, perhaps even naive, experiences of earthly happiness are not what Joseph Campbell had in mind when he spoke of bliss, or even in his treatment of beauty in *The Ecstasy of Being*. The familiar anecdote comes to mind, in which Campbell remarks, "I should have said, 'Follow your blisters.'" Ecstasy, bliss, and beauty are not the easy pleasures that our common use of these words suggest, and the way Campbell describes beauty in this volume can help us unpack this issue.

Campbell concludes that the effective element in all proper art is the rhythm of beauty in which each piece of the art is in harmonious relationship to each other piece, just as each individual piece is to the Whole. That is the challenge for the individual as well, the harmonious relationship to other individuals and each to the Whole, which is not achieved without real suffering in some form. Continuing in this line of thought, Campbell references W. B. Yeats, who suggested that the ideal dramaturgical model "would synthesize the 'pulse of life' with the 'stillness of death.'" Campbell suggests that such a synthesis of opposites is the function of both art and mythology.

The action of synthesizing the pulse of life with the stillness of death necessarily exposes one to existential terrors lying outside the more naive or innocent realms of commonplace beliefs regarding ecstasy, beauty, and bliss. Perhaps it is helpful to think about what Campbell is pointing to as the sublime, though I recognize that the sublime is subject to some of the same naive linguistic problems as bliss, ecstasy, and beauty. A particular problem is that these words commonly convey an added moral dimension. Think of Keats's "Ode on a Grecian Urn" in which he asserts, "'Beauty is truth, truth beauty—that is all ye know on earth, and all ye need to know,'" and perhaps you can sense moral goodness or virtue adhering to the word *beauty*. In fact, the words *beauty, bliss, ecstasy,* and *sublime* are commonly understood as rewards for virtue and morality, and nothing negative may be associated with them. But there is a wealth of philosophical literature on beauty's problematic sibling, the sublime, that helps one understand what's really in play for one who undertakes to follow one's bliss.

There are three thinkers, Pseudo-Longinus, Edmund Burke, and Immanuel Kant, who, taken together, have largely articulated the depths and breadth of the sublime. Burke convincingly insists that terror opens one to the sublime, but he doesn't really demonstrate why the experience of terror is sublime and, like Longinus, he relegates the sublime to the external, natural world. In *The Critique of Judgment*, Kant describes the experience of the sublime as more of an inner experience, much closer to what Campbell called bliss: "Thus, instead of the object, it is rather the cast of mind appreciating it that we have to estimate as sublime." For Kant, the sublime has two main dimensions: one of power and one of magnitude. Sublime encounters are overwhelmingly powerful, and facing them, we are compelled to feel our existential fragility and terror. Additionally, the sublime is of a magnitude so vast that we simply cannot wrap our minds around it. But yet, at some point in the confrontation with the sublime, we recognize that we are a part of it, as it is of us. The sublime reaches into us at the same time we reach into it, and this "mental movement," to use Kant's phrase, begins to lend comprehension to the incomprehensible. It's as if, in an attempt to understand it, we briefly live in the sublime, and it likewise lives in us. Through this mental movement knowledge is generated, and we begin to identify with and partake of the power of the sublime object, transcending our terror and sensing that we are ourselves the origin of the power we face. Campbell has described this as making oneself transparent to the transcendent, and this is what following your bliss is really about. And following your bliss, as Percy Shelly observed regarding the function of the sublime, inevitably persuades us to forsake the easy for the harder pleasures.

THE SECRET CAUSE
(PUBLISHED JUNE 7, 2020)

It's hard to ignore the fact that human life on this planet has been changed by COVID-19, but of course we all know it's not the first time these sorts of changes have happened, nor will it be the last. In fact, in a letter to Oskar Pfister, dated January 27, 1920, Sigmund Freud wrote: "This afternoon we received the news that our sweet Sophie in Hamburg had been snatched away by influenza pneumonia, snatched away in the midst of glowing health, from a full and active life as a competent mother and loving wife, all in four or five days, as though she had never existed."

Freud went on to say that even though they had been worried about Sophie,

> It is so difficult to judge from a distance. And this distance must remain distance; we were not able to travel at once, as we had intended, after the first alarming news; there was no train, not even for an emergency. The undisguised brutality of our time is weighing heavily upon us.

What compassion Freud's words evoke in me, and not just for Freud but for any of us experiencing similar losses in the present. In his book *Thou Art That*, Joseph Campbell writes, "What is central to our considerations is found at that level that rises above that of mere self-preservation. There arises the awakening of compassion, the opening of the human quality in our relationships with both friends and strangers." Compassion is among the most important resources we have right now.

Campbell invokes the Waste Land of the "hideously wounded" Grail King to speak to the circumstances of living that inspire compassion: "The Waste Land is that territory of wounded people—that is, of people living inauthentic lives, broken lives, who have never found the basic energy for living, and they live, therefore, in this blighted landscape." The virus-blighted landscapes of contemporary life present us with a powerful invitation to explore our own inauthentic, broken, or desperate lives, as our sources of distraction and entertainment are curtailed while our illusions of safety and invincibility are shattered by a global pandemic. I am reminded of the line in T. S. Eliot's "The Waste Land": "A crowd flowed over the London Bridge, so many, / I had not thought death had undone so many."

Moving on, getting back to normal, opening up the economy, and recovery are diversions that avoid the scarcely answerable existential and philosophical questions raised by terror and loss. We want answers, we want to understand the causality at work, we want to find the expressway leading away from the Waste Land. We want to deal with the instrumental causes of the pandemic because we are too shaken, too appalled, to accept its secret cause.

We say the cause of the threat to humans is the novel coronavirus, infected bats or pangolins in Wuhan, the pneumonia it causes, or underlying health conditions in its victims; these are certainly instrumental causes. But Campbell advocated for exploring the "secret cause" of things. Articulating his thoughts on this in *Thou Art That*, Campbell suggests that terror "is the emotion that arrests the mind before whatsoever is grave and constant in human suffering and unites it with the secret cause.

What does that mean? That is the key to the whole thing: the secret cause." So what, then, is the secret cause?

Campbell goes on to explain:

> The secret cause of your death is your destiny. Every life has a limitation, and in challenging the limit you are bringing the limit closer to you, and the heroes are the ones who initiate their actions no matter what destiny may result. What happens is, therefore, a function of what the person does. This is true of life all the way through. Here is revealed the secret cause: your own life course is the secret cause of your death.

Death is really a secondary matter to Campbell, primarily because we are all destined to die and how we die is not as important as how we live. When you decide to say yes to your life, yes to everything that animates you, yes to what you're passionate about, yes to what drives you and makes your life significant, when you say yes to all that, careless of how much resistance or pushback you get from the world, you're following your bliss. Campbell isn't suggesting that one be reckless, ignore accepted science, or court danger needlessly; he is simply acknowledging that following one's bliss necessarily exposes one to some sort of suffering. It's not really that complicated: no suffering, no bliss. In fact, Aeschylus teaches us, in *Agamemnon*, about the relationship between *pathos* and *mathos*, suffering and learning, and tells us that we must "suffer, suffer into truth."

When we accept life's invitation to choose the pathway to bliss, Campbell convincingly reminds us that death "is understood as a fulfillment of our life's direction and purpose."

Perhaps it's not the virus that frightens us; perhaps what terrifies us is the chilling realization that we could die having never really lived. And if so, it's an important realization to have, because it's never too late to heed the call to adventure, especially those adventures awaiting us within. It's a question of "do I dare?" Like the J. Alfred Prufrock of T. S. Eliot's eponymous poem, do I dare disturb the Universe?

You Are It *and* It Is Nothing

"Can you make no use of nothing, Nuncle?" Lear may not have been able to make use of nothing, but Joseph Campbell certainly did. In Campbell's book *Myths of Light: Eastern Metaphors of the Eternal*, the idea of nothingness—nothing, no-thingness—is one of the important concepts to grasp:

> What can we say of this strange thing that happens between here and here, so that here there is nothing? You cannot say a thing either is or is not. The things are no things, there is nothing there.

Nothing is a difficult notion to work with; it is antithetical to the sort of materialistic, dualistic thinking to which most of us are accustomed. The nothingness that Campbell refers to is not merely the negation of being, but rather it is the ground of everything, the ground of grounds, since it leads, seduces, or pushes all beings into their limits.

In this volume Campbell tells a delightful story about a young student who is stymied in his attempt to see his guru who lives on the other side of an overflowing, flooded river. The student says, "My teacher is the vehicle of truth to me, he is my god, he is my oracle, I will think about my teacher and I'll walk across the water, and so I did. I thought, "Guru, guru, guru," and he successfully walked across the flooded river atop its engorged waters. Well, the guru was a bit gob smacked by his student's disclosure, and Campbell tells us:

When the student goes, the teacher thinks this was in him. He says, "I'll go to try this thing. I've got to see how this works." So he looks around to see if anybody's watching. When he is sure he is alone, he goes down to the water and looks at the rushing torrent. He thinks, I'm going to do it. He thinks, I, I, I. He steps out onto the river . . . and he sinks like a stone.

The only reason one can walk across water is that there is nobody there; one is pure spirit, spiritus, wind. In Sanskrit, this is prāna. That teacher in the student's mind was a communicator of truth. In his own mind, he was an "I," and an "I" has weight and sinks.

The "I," the ego, can be a problematic psychic organ largely because it is so intransigently subjective and not particularly prone to mindful reflection. Ego psychologists tend to describe ego as the subjective experience we have of ourselves, which is certainly the idea of ego that generally permeates the West and certainly, at least, America. Generally speaking, one's ego provides a way of thinking of oneself as a being in the world and holding a particular perspective of life—a sense of self-familiarity, continuity, and individuality. As Campbell puts it, "an 'I' has weight and sinks." It's as if one's being is a precipitate that falls into the world.

Martin Heidegger had doubts about the efficacy of the concept of ego, pointing out that, contra Descartes, there are more ways of being than simply thinking. The idea of ego wasn't enough for Heidegger; it didn't adequately capture the totality of the being that experiences the world. Therefore, he used the word *Dasein*, which literally means "there-being." Dasein is, as he writes in *The Concept of Time*, "that entity in its Being which we know of as human life; . . . the entity that we each ourselves are, which each of us finds in the fundamental assertion: I am." Heidegger describes *Dasein* as accompanied by a sense of "Throwness," of being thrown into the world regardless of whether we want to be in the world or not. It's rather like Campbell's guru sinking like a stone; it's what happened to the guru, and had to happen to him, despite his fondest wishes.

From where do we sink? From where are we thrown? Campbell says in *Myths of Light* that Being is a great mystery, "beyond which you cannot look." At least for me, this is very similar to Heidegger's Nothingness, which is the ground of everything. Everything is contained in Nothingness, and It projects Being or *Dasein* into the world whether we want to be in the world or not. No-thingness, as Campbell's guru will attest, is not something we can master; we only respond to it.

For Heidegger, *Dasein* is not, in itself, an actuality, but is rather the disclosure of no-thingness. As Campbell put it,

> You are it and it is nothing. It is a very difficult thing to tell anyone about because the words themselves suggest that there is a meaning here, but the thing is just to get it, and that is why you can't communicate or teach [it]: you can only bring a person up to it.

Asian mythologies are remarkably compatible with Heidegger's philosophy. In each, Nothing and no-thingness are not negations, but the language they use is often hard to grasp. However, it is "awfully easy," Campbell says, "to sympathize with and go with because anything you are doing is it [...] and you realize that the whole mystery and void is shining through at you, you are there."

THE FESTIVAL *of* PASSING FORMS

The title of Campbell's *Masks of God* series engages one immediately. We all want to know what is behind the mask; we want to lift the veil and peer behind the often uncanny, enigmatic façade of life. And if you live somewhere long enough, and pay attention closely enough, you can't help but discover at least a few of the many rich layers of history living (sometimes literally) just below the surface of your daily comings and goings. There is a sense of the immemorial always within reach, and I never fail to be touched by the whispering echoes of ancient voices that spoke, sang, laughed, wept, hoped, and shouted more than a millennium ago in and around Flagstaff, AZ, the city I've called home for nearly thirty years.

The earliest habitation of the American Southwest dates to before 11000 BP—an astonishingly ancient date, and these early humans were presumably hunters. (Perhaps even more astonishingly, on December 1, 2020, *Smithsonian* magazine ran a story about the discovery of tens of thousands of painted images, dating to around 12000 BP, along eight miles of cliff walls in the Amazon rainforest.) Eventually, the inhabitants of the Colorado Plateau developed a genius for masonry and agriculture, created impressive architecture, and grew crops of maize, beans, squash, and even cotton by conceiving ingenious irrigation systems that mitigated the harsh growing conditions of the arid climate.

Even though the community was permanently abandoned by the early 1200's C.E., there is something ineffable that remains, some . . . experience . . . that one may have standing in the reconstructed ball court or peering through a window of a partially collapsed wall at Wupatki. Roaming around such places, a murky prehistory tickles the imagination. It comes alive with images of families, young men and women, leaders, storytellers, the elderly, all going about their daily lives, their routines, work, and recreations. I imagine that they, like ourselves, hardly gave a thought to the inevitability that one day life as they knew it would end, that their people would disappear, and what they saw and heard and felt and believed would, in some unimaginably distant time, become the subject of abstract conjecture. Because they were preliterate and left no history, memoir, or cultural criticism, their fate has been consigned to the realm of speculation based on climate data and autochthonous remnants of the excavated communal trash heap.

Of course, it's wrong to say that sometime after the beginning of the thirteenth century the people who created Wupatki mysteriously disappeared. I'm sure their emigration was no mystery to them, and in fact they continue to live on in their descendants: thirteen different Native American communities consider Wupatki to be a sacred site, have a significant oral tradition regarding the area, and claim ancestral ties to the site.

A lack of a written history should not bamboozle one into believing that the inhabitants of ancient sites like Wupatki were unsophisticated, crude people living in a disorganized, undeveloped society. In fact, they seemed to engage in a sophisticated trade economy. Scarlet macaw remains have been found on site, and there is also evidence that they traded with other groups from the Pacific Ocean to the Lower Mississippi and Gulf Coast regions. These were smart, cosmopolitan, adventurous, and creative people, and I think that their fundamental concerns about life must have been very similar to our own. However, we don't often recognize our commonality because we simply don't reflect upon the antiquity of the ideas (agriculture, wheels, levers, varieties of fire) we live with every day. If we can see these ancients as ourselves, we bring the idea of them "to life as our own," Campbell writes in *The Masks of God, Volume 1: Primitive Mythology,* "in the way . . . of wonder—sympathetic, instructive delight; not judging morally, but participating with our own awakened humanity in the festival of the passing forms."

Contrary to our will or desire, we are, in the first quarter of the twenty-first century, often left to wonder what life means and how we should live. Our estrangement from the world, from one another, and from ourselves, not to mention our history, has become too deep, and too often malignantly cruel. We're not separate from the world, and we often forget that we don't, as Alan Watts has said, come into this world but come out of it. The earth influences us in the same way children are influenced by their parents. How then are we to live, and what is life's point? Mythologies try to provide answers, but read too literally they only serve to deepen the estrangement.

Joseph Campbell often remarked that what we're really looking for is the experience of being alive. That's no small thing; it's not always a simple or pleasant task, because it means saying yes to absolutely all of life. The experience of being alive transcends meanings and purposes, it concentrates the mind and triggers the imagination, the architect of most human behavior, and it connects us to our world, one another, the present, the future, and the past; who we are, who we will become, and who we have been; as well as to those ancient peoples who inhabit the "dark backward and abysm" of time. If there must be a point to life, then let it be simply this: to participate with one's full humanity in the festival of passing forms, while somehow continuing to be mindful that one of those passing forms is oneself.

THE INFINITE REACH *of* MERCY

The still point is a poetic image that Joseph Campbell remarks upon several times in his book *The Inner Reaches of Outer Space: Metaphor as Myth and as Religion*. Referenced only four times in T. S. Eliot's, "The Four Quartets," and only then in "Burnt Norton," the first of the quartets, the phrase, "still point"— especially when it appears as "the still point of the turning world"— remains inexhaustibly evocative. But before we discuss anything else, metaphor demands our attention. Judging from the title of this volume of Campbell's work, metaphor is itself metaphoring as myth and religion.

To understand the necessity of use of the word *metaphor* in Campbell's title, one must understand the word in its nonallegorical sense: as *metapherein*, meaning "to transfer." Hannah Arendt deftly and beautifully explains this in her introduction to *Illuminations: Essays and Reflections* by Walter Benjamin:

> For a metaphor establishes a connection which is sensually perceived in its immediacy and requires no interpretation, while an allegory always proceeds from an abstract notion and then invents something palpable to represent it almost at will. The allegory must be explained before it can become meaningful, a solution must be found to the riddle it presents, so the often laborious interpretation of allegorical figures always unhappily reminds one of the solving of puzzles even when no more ingenuity is demanded than in the allegorical representation of death by a skeleton. . . .

Metaphors are the means by which the oneness of
the world is poetically brought about.

This rhetorical transference gives the invisible realm material
form, and thereby "the still point of the turning world" makes
itself available to be experienced. "It is there," Campbell says
of the still point, "which is no 'where,' that the Eye opens of
Transcendent Vision."

Eliot prefaces his quartets with two quotes from Heraclitus,
the last of which is self-evidently paradoxical: "The way upward
and the way downward are the same." What does it mean that
so much paradox is present in this particular work?

> At the still point of the turning world.
>> Neither flesh nor fleshless;
> Neither from nor towards;
>> at the still point, there the dance is,
> But neither arrest nor movement.
>> And do not call it fixity,
> Where past and future are gathered.
>> Neither movement from nor towards,
> Neither ascent nor decline.
>> Except for the point, the still point,
> There would be no dance,
>> and there is only the dance

The use of paradox as a literary device is a way of disclosing unexpected hidden, perhaps even nonrational, profound
truths. In *Niels Bohr: His Life and Work*, Hans Bohr quoted
his father saying that there are two sorts of truths: a "profound

truth [is] recognized by the fact that the opposite is also a profound truth, in contrast to trivialities where opposites are obviously absurd." Bohr touches on an important point: the deep
questions life raises, its insoluble mysteries, the unanswerable
ontological questions that trouble sleep and keep one staring
at the bedroom ceiling at 3:00 a.m., are redolent with the par-
adoxes of living. When one encounters paradox in literature,
especially poetry, one senses art imitating life, for life itself is
seldom logical, often paradoxical, and, more often than not,
unfathomable. Paradox provokes a seizure of the intellect,
which then pivots one to a more pensive, inquisitive state of
mind. Paradox seems to insist upon imaginative, experimental,
unconventional thinking, and problem-solving.

At the conclusion of *The Inner Reaches of Outer Space*,
Campbell quotes from Romans 11:32 ("For God has bound
everyone over to disobedience so that he may have mercy on
them all"), and asks, "How far does one's mercy reach?" He
answers his own question saying, "For only so far do the inner
and the outer worlds meet." This is another paradox, yes? The
point at which the inner and outer worlds meet would necessarily be neither, or perhaps both, inner or outer. Yet it is here,
amid paradox, where once again we find the still point of the
turning world.

Plato writes, in *Timaeus*, that within the soul was formed the
"corporeal universe, and brought the two together and united
them center to center. The soul, interfused everywhere from
the center to the circumference of heaven, of which also she is
the external envelopment, *herself turning in herself*" (emphasis is
mine). Thus the entire Cosmos is ensouled and, as Plato recounts
in the *Republic*, wheels around another image of a still point, the

Spindle of Necessity (the Myth of Er describes the spindle and its governess, Necessity, the great goddess whose daughters are the Fates). In Plato's conceptualization, the soul may be thought of as motion made manifest; after all, the Latin word for soul is *anima*, from which we derive the word *animate*, and we may conclude that self-motion is a characteristic of anything with a soul. And thus infused, the entire universe wheels, centrifugally, out of Soul or, its Greek homonym, *psyche* (ψυχή).

Following from Campbell, one may conclude that mercy inhabits the point at which the inner and outer worlds meet, Plato's point of singularity at which Soul suffuses the entire corporeal universe and becomes infinite. Again then, how far does mercy reach? Its reach must be regarded as infinite, and thankfully so, because we've never needed it more.

WHOSOEVER LOSES THEIR LIFE WILL FIND IT

In *The Inner Reaches of Outer Space: Metaphor as Myth and Religion*, Joseph Campbell writes that the mythic metaphor, the mythic image, "is necessarily physical and thus apparently of outer space. The inherent connotation is always, however, psychological and metaphysical, which is to say, of inner space." Psychologically, then, what are we to make of the chilling mythological rituals and images of human—or animal, for that matter—sacrifice?

In a 1971 lecture to his Sarah Lawrence class, Professor Campbell described what he called the basic myth of the Neolithic culture, which is that there was "a time when there was no time, a mythological age" in which beings were "neither human nor animal, nor plant; a kind of mixing of forms." There was no death or birth, and this age came to an end with the "Mythological Event," the killing of one of these beings. Campbell is pointing to the idea that when this generous understanding of existence as being is simply another thing among the vast, untold number of things, it is simply one thing no more important than another, and something experienced with absolutely no separation from the natural world at all. When that being is betrayed, death and hunger enter the world.

One of those beings was cut up and buried, and from the buried parts the food plant emerged. Therefore, what you're eating is your relative, something very close to you, something of which you were once a part until the psychological development of the individual, subjective ego—a state of consciousness that emphasizes separateness and inescapable subjectivity—is undertaken.

Professor Campbell points out that the gruesome rituals of human sacrifice belonging to some planting cultures are literal reenactments of the primal murder and the subsequent boon of a dietary staple. The sacrificial victim is to be understood as the god or goddess who, by offering itself to death, functions as a somewhat more literal Eucharist, ensuring the continued well-being of the community. Additionally, the ritual killing seems to function as atonement (at-one-ment) with the nature of things both immanent and transcendent. Indeed, it is filled with the energies of the cosmos itself.

Campbell writes in *Inner Reaches* that "if the witness is prepared, there ensues a transfer of self-identification from the temporal, reflecting body to the . . . eternal source, and one then knows oneself as consubstantial with what is of no time or place but universal and beyond death, yet incarnate in all beings everywhere and forever." Such a sacrifice leaves, theoretically at least, no individual or cultural guilt. These rituals created a *temenos*, a sacred space within which, through the act of sacrifice, one is returned to a mythic age, an age which is not located in some distant, murky past but exists right here in the present.

What is clear, whether we choose to discuss sacrifice in literal or in symbolic, mythic terms, is that we are discussing an act of violence. However, sacred violence is different from, shall we say, random or profane violence. Sacrifice makes an act of violence sacred, which in a different setting, a setting devoid of tradition and the intentionally constructed *temenos*, would simply be a violation of law or taboo. Another quality that a sacrifice must possess is that of meaningfulness. Events like the Vietnam War, 9/11, or the ongoing pandemic weigh heavily upon cultural consciousness because so many people died for no apparent good or just cause.

The way in which we talk about sacrifice matters, and a fair amount of categorical debate often surrounds the framing of a sacrificial act. For example: Did Jesus offer himself as a willing sacrifice, or was he executed by the state as a criminal? Indeed, both narratives may be, and have in fact been, argued. But I want to return to Joseph Campbell's notion that the mythic image, the mythological act of sacrifice, even though it may be described as a physical, material, and external act, is also necessarily psychological and metaphysical, lest we become fixated on the ethics and morality of the mythological act without understanding the psychological impact.

What is, then, the psychological impact of the mythological motif of sacrifice? In *Psychology and Religion: West and East*, C. G. Jung suggests that what we're sacrificing is a self-interested, physicalist perspective, a perspective of the ego that compels one to think that they are only this material form, beyond which lies only oblivion:

> What I sacrifice is my own selfish claim, and by doing this I give up myself. Every sacrifice is therefore, to a greater or lesser degree, a self-sacrifice. The degree to which it is so depends on the significance of the gift. If it is of great value to me and touches my most personal feelings, I can be sure that in giving up my egoistic claim I shall challenge my ego personality to revolt. I can also be sure that the power which

suppresses this claim, and thus suppresses me, must be the self. Hence it is the self that causes me to make the sacrifice; nay more, it compels me to make it. The self is the sacrificer, and I am the sacrificed gift, the human sacrifice.

When an individual compels the sacrifice of another, say, as Abraham compels Isaac, one must at some level, Jung points out, "feel the knife [enter] into his own breast" and become "at the same time the sacrificer and the sacrificed." What good do we get from it? What we gain from the sacrifice is ourselves, resurrected and renewed, newly possessed of all the things in us that were previously scattered, never properly related, or objectively witnessed—and as Campbell has often remarked, we may become transparent to the transcendent. The sacrifice facilitates the transformation of suffering into a creative force. To gloss the poet Wendell Berry, we get to have love in our hearts.

The Greatest Poem
Is Lyric Life Itself

In *The Masks of God, Volume 2: Oriental Mythology,* Joseph Campbell quotes from *Gitagovinda (The Song of the Cowherd)* by the poet Jayadeva: "Oh may this poem . . . delight all lover's hearts." The poet and artist Lawrence Ferlinghetti, who delighted the hearts of all lovers (and delighted the lovers of great hearts too), died on February 22, 2021. He's already been eulogized in a multitude of ways, and with language that far exceed any bon mots that I might muster, but I do want to consider something he said in the *New York Times* "Last Word" feature of the online obituaries section. When I heard it, it rang in my soul like a bell.

"Last Word" is a series of short on-camera interviews featuring prominent figures reflecting upon their own lives. The footage is released only with the individual's obituary. Ferlinghetti's piece was extraordinarily intimate, and allows one to witness the intelligence, the heartfulness, the passions, and the sensitivities of a man who managed to forge his life in the flames of creativity and courage. In this video, Ferlinghetti tells us his early life was "unhappy" and remarks "so I escaped by lyricism." He goes on to say, "When present day life gets too awful, there's the lyric escape." Ferlinghetti follows up with a few examples of the lyric escape, such as writing a poem, looking at the moon, or even "shacking up with your best girl-friend," but mostly I hear, embedded deep in his words, that the lyric escape is a flight into beauty.

And it's not just any beauty, it's the beauty found within. It is an "enchanted mood," Herman Melville insists in *Moby Dick*, in which "thy spirit ebbs away to whence it came;

becomes diffused through time and space; like Cranmer's sprinkled Pantheistic ashes, forming at last a part of every shore the round globe over." (As an aside, Melville is referring to Thomas Cranmer, the Archbishop of Canterbury, who was ordered burned to death by Queen Mary on March 21, 1556.) Both Ferlinghetti's lyric escape and Melville's enchanted mood refer to the aesthetic arrest by which one is overcome in the presence of deep beauty.

Ferlinghetti seems to know that deep beauty, the goal of the lyric escape, is the antidote to life's pain. Readers of Joseph Campbell will be familiar with his discussions regarding James Joyce's theory of art, in which proper art induces in the beholder a seizure of the heart, an aesthetic arrest. I've always thought Joyce's seizure of the heart to involve at least some small degree of physical pain, a cardiac event induced by an intense psychological experience. People end up on emergency-room gurneys for similar reasons all the time. Perhaps because we discover some modicum of pain in the experience of it, beauty has a salutary, restorative effect when we find ourselves in the grip of the pain of living. Beauty functions as a homeopathic remedy for the pain of living; it's the healing alchemy of like curing like.

Beauty, as Rilke puts it, is "the beginning of terror"; we know we must eventually take our leave of "this earth of majesty, this blessed plot," this place where piercing beauty makes its home, and that either it or ourselves will eventually turn to ashes. In his beguilingly titled book *Essays in Idleness*, the fourteenth-century Zen monk-poet Yoshida Kenkō captures the essential impermanence of beauty in a poignant, elegant meditation: "If we lived forever, never to vanish like the dews of Adashino, never to fade like the crematory smoke on Toribeyama, men would scarcely feel the beauty of things" (my translation).

Containing both gratification and pain, beauty transcends dualities and remains within the sphere of eternity, not only beyond the veil of time and space but beyond pleasure and pain, beyond joy and sorrow, beyond life and death.

The lyric escape transformed Dante's pain of exile into the *Divina Commedia*, the *Divine Comedy*. The same year he was diagnosed with tuberculosis, Keats's lyric escape created "Ode on a Grecian Urn," a lyric flight that allowed him to live for a precious while within a timeless, evergreen scene etched on an ancient urn where young lovers loved forever, leaves never fell from trees, and he remained "the foster child of silence and slow time." In bed after yet another bout with influenza and brittle mental health, Virginia Woolf's lyric escape writes herself out of infirmity with the archly beautiful essay "On Being Ill." Lying there, she imagines herself a deserter from "the army of the upright" looking up to see the "extraordinary" and "strangely overcoming" spectacle of the "divinely beautiful" and "also divinely heartless" sky that healthy, perpendicular people seldom notice.

"With the hook of life still in us still we must wriggle," Woolf writes. "Left to ourselves we speculate thus carnally. We need the poets to imagine for us. The duty of Heaven-making should be attached to the office of Poet Laureate." Perhaps so. I'd like to think I'd feel at home in a heaven imagined by Billy Collins or Elizabeth Bishop. But the duty of Heaven-making unfailingly falls to each one of us, and it's a duty made lighter if we learn the art of the lyric escape. After all, as Ferlinghetti wrote in *Poetry as Insurgent Art*, "the greatest poem is lyric life itself."

FLIRTING *with* REALITY:
AT PLAY *in the* PLAY *of the* WORLD

One of the things that I find endearing about Joseph
Campbell is that frequently in his writing, as well as his lectures, he displays a palpable enthusiasm for certain subjects.
When I read *Myths of Light: Eastern Metaphors of the Eternal*,
for example, I recognize Campbell's enthusiasm in its tru-
est sense—enthusiasm as it's derived from the Greek word
entheos, which is to be rapt or enthralled, divinely inspired,
or possessed by a god—when he speaks on the subject of
jiva, or life force, the animating principle, a principle he
called "the deathless soul."

Once, struggling to come up with a metaphor that might
more easily facilitate an understanding of the deathless soul,
Campbell was inspired by common ceiling lights:

> Each bulb carries the light. We can think of this
> totality as many bulbs; this is the lunar world of mul-
> tiple entities. On the other hand we can focus on the
> one light that emanates from all the bulbs. This is
> the solar consciousness. What are we focusing on, the
> light or the lights? Which way of looking at things
> is correct? If one bulb breaks, we take it out and put
> another in—is it the bulb that's important or is it the
> light? Then I said to the boys, "Now I look down here
> and I see all your heads like bulbs and within them
> is consciousness. What's important: this particular
> head or the consciousness that's in it?"

In Western mythologies, and as far as Western thought generally regards human beings, we tend to focus on the importance of individual bulbs, so to speak, while Asian mythologies regard the light as the most important thing. For Asia, generally speaking, it is the *élan vital*, as Henri Bergson called it, that vital principle that strays, vanishes, returns, and animates each living thing, that is truly worthy of awe.

"The idea," Campbell writes, "of the reincarnating principle is thus of two orders: first, the reincarnating principle that puts on bodies and puts them off as the Moon puts on and puts off its light body; and the other is that principle of sheer light that never dies, the light that is incarnate and immanent in all." The solar light that never dies, reflected in the lunar cycles of waxing and waning luminosity characterizing the *élan vital*, can be seen to be involved in a type of play which, in turn, bestows the aspects of a game to life. In a recent episode of the JCF podcast *Pathways with Joseph Campbell*, I commented on Campbell's remarks regarding the peculiar tendency of the human being to find itself through imitation: children imitate parents, hunting cultures wear animal masks and skins in imitation of the sacred totem animal, and planting cultures bury their dead in the ground as if expecting a new life to sprout. Reflecting on these mimesises Campbell said, "At some point you have to wonder: To what degree is this a game?" Realizing that life is a game or a performance helps us remember that we're actors who have forgotten we're in a play. Shakespeare, in *As You Like It*, writes, "All the world's a stage, and all the men and women merely players; they have their exits and their entrances, and one man in his life plays many parts." We star in comedies, tragedies, melodramas, and farce; from one moment to the next we are men, women, or children; heroes, villains, victims, lovers, or fools. The nature of life reveals itself to us in *spiel raum*, the realm of play.

Eugen Fink put it this way in *Play as Symbol of the World: And Other Writings*:

> Play comes to be a "cosmic metaphor" for the total appearance and disappearance of existing things in the time-space of the world. The frothing, intoxicated tide of life, which elevates living beings in the delight in reproducing, is secretly one with the dark surge that drags the living down into death. Life and death, birth and dying, womb and tomb are twinned: it is the same moving force of the totality that brings forth and annihilates, that begets and kills, that unites the highest delight and the deepest grief.

A failure to understand the rules of the game or its objective has never been a hindrance to playing it; children often make up rules as they go along, or they play by very fluid rules that, contrary to spoiling the game, enhance it and make the game more expressive, more relevant to a particular moment, more delightful. A childlike immersion in the game is indispensable. In Greek, play is *paizo*, and it's what a child (*pais*) does. Fink invokes fragment 52 of Heraclitus, which says, *"Aion pais esti paizōn, pesseuōn; paidos hē basileiē"* or "Lifetime [more properly, Time itself] is a child at play, moving pieces in a game. Kingship belongs to the child." Contemplating this fragment, the awareness begins to dawn that the child may be moving pieces in a game she may not understand, moving the pieces randomly, or making up moves as she goes along, and yet within the context of the game the child is always and in all ways, as Hamlet said, the king of infinite space.

Realizing that the universe is at play, and that play is the ground of being humans occupy, we can, as Campbell puts it, achieve an "undifferentiated consciousness while awake." Viewed as a game, life ceases to be unrelenting drudgery, hard labor, or pointless because the point is the game itself. At that point of undifferentiated consciousness, Professor Campbell says there are two choices: "You may let the body drop off, close the eyes, as it were, and unite with this central transcendent realization. Or you may open the eyes and take delight in the play of forms, seeing through them the one form. That is the attitude of world affirmation, the affirmation of every single thing, even the monsters."

A LOVER'S QUARREL *with the* WORLD

In Chapter IV of *The Masks of God, Volume 2: Oriental Mythology,*
Joseph Campbell supplies his readers with a quote from the
Buddha's Fire Sermon, a dharma talk focused on renunciation
and developing an "aversion" to the material world, including
expressions of the self in body, mind, and imagination:

> And in conceiving this aversion, he becomes divested of
> passion, and by the absence of passion he becomes free,
> and when he is free he becomes aware that he is free;
> and he knows that rebirth is exhausted, that he has
> lived the holy life, that he has done what it behooved
> him to do, and that he is no more for this world.

One gets the sense that "this sorrowful world," as Campbell
refers to it, "will go on forever," and as a result, there appears
to be a powerful religious instinct to escape suffering by leaving the world and physical, biological life entirely. Lifetime
after lifetime of ascetic practice is designed to burn off karma
and blow out the flame of life, ending the cycles of death and
rebirth by reaching nirvana, which literally means blowing
out or quenching. The negation of earthly life isn't unique
to Asian religious traditions; Christianity similarly disparages
the material world and worldly existence, and looks beyond
it to an eternal life in heaven spent in the presence of God.
In a very, very broad sense, the main difference between the
two is that Christianity, lacking the eternally recurring and
reincarnating life monad, limits rebirth to a transformation
of consciousness.

I can't help but conclude that the life negating reflex exhibited in most religions is evoked by a literalization of mythology. If one participates completely, unquestioningly, in religious life, the narratives and symbols of the religion must be understood to be literally true, historically real, and ultimately irrefutable. In such a cast of mind, the world and worldliness is bad, fallen, a prison. The world is often problematic for human beings, it is true, but it is also true that the world's ubiquitous beauty, its inexhaustible stores of wonder, dazzles the soul and confounds understanding.

I sometimes find myself longing for a reengagement with the Renaissance ideals of Giambattista Vico's humanism, for example, or with Marsilio Ficino's explorations of consciousness. I long for enthusiastic, one might even say joyful, textual criticism, and the re-emergence of the primacy of aesthetic ideals. I still yearn for what Lionel Trilling called "the old classical culture, that wonderful imagined culture of the ancient world which no one but school boys, schoolmasters, scholars, and poets believe in" (*Beyond Culture: Essays on Literature and Learning*). I agree with Trilling. I know full well that my romanticized fantasy of classical life never existed in reality in the way in which it lives in my imagination.

Certainly there exists a middle way between a hopeless, passive resignation to life and *Sallekhana*, a means of self-destruction that simultaneously destroys karma and the possibility of rebirth by suppressing, and ultimately abandoning, all physical and mental activities. It's not that I can't see logic at work in the practice of *Sallekhana*; in fact, I do. The deliberate negation of life suggests that there is at least a modicum of humanity beyond the reach of institutional and cultural control, and that this residue of unadulterated, incorruptible humanity, small and unappreciated though it may be, serves as a critique of culture, a criticism of life itself, and prevents life lived in the agora from becoming all-consuming, overdetermining, and imperiously monolithic. The horrifying sight of Buddhist monks self-immolating during the Vietnam War remains, perhaps, the most poignant of examples.

However, living outside of these religious traditions, this ultimate self-abnegation seems so extreme as to contradict religious tenets of ahimsa, prohibitions against causing injury or death to any living creature. But there is an argument to be made from within the tradition that this severity is a part of one's ethical and moral effort to know what is real, to seize reality from the powerful grip of illusion and desire. But I fail to be persuaded by these arguments because, at the heart of the matter, self-annihilation necessarily prohibits transformation of the self and by extension the world.

Beings who are spiritually awakened share their gifts with others who, in turn, are transformed, and eventually their transformation transforms others in kind and leads to the transformation of the world. In his novel *Howards End*, E. M. Forster wrote, "Death destroys a man, but the idea of death saves him." It is the idea of death, not actual death itself, that is redemptive. The idea of death saves one from the loss of self demanded by the dehumanized activities institutions and the materialistic beliefs of a culture or society precisely because it concentrates the mind on what is most significant about human existence: its loves, its passions, its triumphs, its beautiful failures, and its human—all-too-human—frailties.

Samuel Taylor Coleridge believed that the willing suspension of disbelief constitutes poetic faith. Incidentally, it also constitutes scientific methodology, technological innovation, and especially mythological thought. Suspending disbelief means that we set aside our own beliefs and consider possibilities that previously we had been unable to imagine. Thinking in the metaphors of myth rather than the reified literalisms of religious dogma reveals not mere arguments from authority or appeals to faith but the activated symbols, clues, and personal intuitions that can take one to the brink of transcendent states. The truths we receive from mythology are revelations about what it means to be a human being; they are revelations of life itself. To make use of those truths, we must remain engaged in life *as it is*. If we negate or manage to escape life, we forfeit those truths.

In his "Ninth Duino Elegy," Rainer Maria Rilke (translation by Stephen Mitchell) put it this way:

> But because truly being here is so much; because everything here
>   apparently needs us, this fleeting world, which
>   in some strange way
> keeps calling to us. Us, the most fleeting of all.
> Once for each thing. Just once; no more. And we too,
> just once. And never again. But to have been
> this once, completely, even if only once:
> to have been at one with the earth, seems
>   beyond undoing.

VIRTUE *and* DEMOCRACY

Given that the health of democracy around the world seems to be ailing, it might be interesting to explore what Occidental mythology, and Greek thought in particular, might say to us about this aspect of contemporary life. In a 2010 White House speech, President Obama remarked:

> And so it was that the democratic example of a small group of city-states more than two thousand years ago could inspire the founding generation of this country, that led one early American to imagine that "the days of Greece may be revived in the woods of America."
>
> It's the sense of nobility and morality written in the pages of those timeless Greek texts, which have instructed students . . . down the ages, in every corner of the world.

That same sense of nobility and morality influenced Thomas Jefferson and inspired his humanism and his belief that the human goal of happiness could be achieved through the cultivation of virtue, particularly nobility and reason, which the Greeks called *arete*. In *The Masks of God, Volume 3: Occidental Mythology*, Joseph Campbell defines *arete* as "pride in excellence, which has been called the very soul of the Homeric hero—as it is the soul, also, of the Celtic and Germanic; or, indeed, everywhere, of the unbroken [individual]." Jefferson believed that natural rights, emphasizing reason rather than divine providence, are the claim of humankind. The "rational study of the world as a field of facts" contributes to the understanding that humankind is not a product of, and therefore not subject to, some particular god, but is rather a product of nature. As such, it is limited only by nature itself and fate, which may simply be the word we assign to the perennially enshrouded, stubbornly incomprehensible operations of the universe. And yet, despite some profound limitations, a startling degree of freedom waits to be discovered through an empirical engagement with the world.

As Joseph Campbell put it, in his beautifully poetic way:

> The rational study of the world as a field of facts to be observed began, as we all know, with the Greeks. For when they kissed their fingers at the moon, or at rosy-fingered dawn, they did not fall on their faces before it, but approached it, man to man, or man to goddess—and what they found was already what we have found: that all is indeed wonderful, yet submissive to examination.

Jefferson acquired much of his personal philosophy from the Greek Stoics. From the Latin historians, he derived much of his political philosophy. Those influences continue to shape the country which he helped to create. It seems to me that contemporary America has the structure and temperament of ancient Rome (especially late imperial Rome), yet her aspirational ideals always seem to lean toward Athens. Clearly, Jefferson disliked the idea of what he called an artificial aristocracy, but he did subscribe to the notion of a natural aristocracy. In an 1813 letter to John Adams he writes, "There is a natural aristocracy among men. The grounds of this are virtue [*arete*] and talents."

Greek democracy in the classical age lasted a surprisingly short time, from around 507 BCE to 404 BCE when Sparta defeated Athens in the Peloponnesian War and installed an oligarchy of wealthy collaborationist Athenians to rule Athens. The Thirty Tyrants were overthrown in 403 BCE, and an attenuated democracy was restored until finally, in 338, when Alexander and his father Phillip II conquered Athens, it was destroyed. There is no single reason for the collapse of Athenian democracy, but I think the self-righteous thrill of the egoic hunger for power present—for example, in the execution of Socrates in 399 BCE—played no small part.

There is little doubt that a significant factor in the arrest and execution of Socrates was that he had become, in his own words (according to Plato), a gadfly, an exasperating pain in the . . . er, neck, whose self-identified purpose was to stir the "noble steed" of Athens to life. Socrates was generally critical of Athenian politicians and power brokers and indeed of democracy itself (he had close relationships with at least a few of the Thirty Tyrants). For decades it had been his habit to expose pompous or powerful Athenians who claimed to possess special status as poseurs, publicly exposing and humiliating them, thereby inspiring deep, burning resentments that compensated feelings of profound shame and inferiority. In turn, the powerful naturally looked for opportunities to remove agitators and limit speech, eroding democratic ideals and practices.

Aristophanes, a comic playwright, lampooned Socrates in his play *The Clouds* as the trivial, eccentric headmaster of a sophist academy called "The Thinkery." But Socrates isn't the

play's only target of satire; Strepsiades is Aristophanes's caricature of the average dull, entitled, lazy Athenian, a Gleasonesque
character reminiscent of a Ralph Kramden–like self-saboteur
always looking for an edge or advantage or a way to get something for nothing. After Strepsiades's scheme, aided by what
his son learns at The Thinkery, backfires, Strepsiades burns the
school down.

The exposure of casually corrupt and malignantly narcissistic self-interests, paired with the force multiplier of public humiliation, has throughout history been the match that
touches off the most destructive conflagrations of societies. In
a culture where individuals are only interested in themselves,
the cultivation of power and acts of violence remain the only
bases for human relationships, and its most precious freedoms
are forfeited along with the ideals of democracy.

In the introduction to *Phaedo* in the *Delphi Complete
Works of Plato*, the philosopher Simmias is quoted as saying
that we have a duty to face the truth and follow it wherever
it leads us even if, perhaps especially if, we don't like it: "And
if truth divine and inspired is not to be had, then let a man
take the best of human notions, and upon this frail bark let
him sail through life." So perhaps, as we near 250 years since
the signing of the Declaration of Independence, we can take a
moment to relish the novel, ambitious, and demanding idea of
Jeffersonian democracy and resolve to sail upon its frail bark
toward the best human notions of genuine freedom, civility,
and compassion.

THE HEALING INTEGRITY *of* LOVE

There is much to like about Joseph Campbell's *Romance of the Grail: The Magic and Mystery of Arthurian Myth*, and it contains, to quote from *Zorba the Greek*, "everything, the full catastrophe." But for now, I'm mostly curious to look at the way suffering and healing is treated in the Arthurian romances and, by extension, in mythology in general.

The Arthurian romances aren't merely legends or literary works; taken as a whole, they reflect an entire chivalric age. This age seems increasingly distant or fanciful to contemporary readers, an epic period in which honor, nobility, truthfulness, and fidelity call forth a wondrous, enchanted world. It teems with extravagantly impossible challenges, which are, in the end, made entirely possible. Contradiction and confusion are baked into the Grail legends; they operate in this literature much in the same way consciousness itself operates, teaching the reader that what is omitted, what is left out or repressed, always returns to unsettle every settled interpretation, no matter how monolithic it may at first seem.

Initial failure is a necessary feature of the Grail quest, and that's why the Grail hero is inevitably a callow, naive, inexperienced youth, a beginner in over his head. The beginner's mind is of the utmost importance because for a beginner there are a multitude of possibilities; for an expert, there are few. Because beginners often fail, they are able to remain open to constant questioning, improvisation, and revision, qualities that are indispensable when dealing with phenomena that can never be fully known or adequately represented by human beings. Professor Campbell addresses this in *Romance of the Grail*:

The goal of the Grail hero is to heal that wound, but he is to do so without knowing how he is to do so. He is to be a perfect innocent, not to know the rules of the quest, and he is to ask spontaneously, "What is the matter?"

The quest begins in earnest only after the hero has failed in his first, unintentional visit to the Grail Castle and commits to returning to it in order to fulfill, as Jessie Weston notes in *The Quest of the Holy Grail*, "the conditions which shall qualify him to obtain a full knowledge of the marvels he has beheld." Epistemological narcissism, unreflected certainty, and dogma snuff out innocence and provoke the Grail Castle to disappear even farther into the metaphysical mists.

Fully immersed in the initiatory situation, the innocent quester is progressively introduced to suffering, his own and that of others. Suffering is among the most important symbols in the Grail romances. Arthurian romances and mythology in general are not very prescriptive when it comes to disease and physical suffering. Rather, myth largely focuses on learning to see through our physical suffering to the spiritual malaise that afflicts us. It is as if that when the soul suffers, the body cries out.

The Grail King suffers from a *parmi les cuisses*, and his suffering is directly related to the wasting away of all that he oversees. This phrase *parmi les cuisses* (literally meaning "among the thighs") is a euphemism for a wound to the genitals. This association has its roots in a belief, shared by many cultures in antiquity, that semen was produced in several places in the body, including the marrow of the thigh bone. That and the thigh's proximity to the testicles resulted in a close association between thighs and the male genitalia. It is, however, crucial to remember that there are always two orders or levels to consider when reading myth: the lower order deals with the more literal aspects of material existence, like the creative principles of fertility and generation, choice and action, and physical birth and death. The higher order deals with the mysteries of spiritual renewal and revivification, spiritual death and rebirth. A wound to the genitalia is, from this perspective, very different from the cringe-inducing image of a physical wound.

For example, both Odysseus and Captain Ahab suffer from *parmi les cuisses*. Odysseus has a scar on his thigh where he was gored by a boar when he was a boy, and in his later life it revealed his identity. Odysseus's scarred-over wound symbolically constellates the defenselessness, disarray, and destruction of his home and property by the hungry bivouacked suitors. The thigh scar presages his twenty-year disappearance, the lonely confinement of his wife, and the self-doubting son deprived of a father's instruction. And Ahab didn't merely lose his leg to Moby Dick; Ishmael tells us:

> For it had not been very long prior to the Pequod's sailing from Nantucket, that he had been found one night lying prone upon the ground, and insensible; by some unknown, and seemingly inexplicable, unimaginable casualty, his ivory limb having been so violently displaced, that it had stake-wise smitten, and all but pierced his groin."

In Moby Dick, Ahab's wound is tied to the scarcity of whale sightings, the frequent tide-overs, the onboard mishaps, his own emotional and physical isolation from his young wife, their new child, his crew, and ultimately the emptiness of his own heart. Physical wounding in myth is a symbol of spiritual suffering.

Compassion is what heals such a wound, not diagnosis, prescriptions for medication, or surgery. The suffering is relieved by asking, in all sincere innocence, a question, the answer to which cannot be known by the questioner: "Uncle, what ails thee?" This healing question is the therapeutic move, the healing application of compassion: You tell me what is wrong because I can't know, and when you tell me, I will stand in that suffering with you until you discover that you can bear it. Joseph Campbell writes that it is through Parzival's "integrity in love that he finally becomes the Grail King and heals Anfortas and the land." What better way to describe compassion than integrity in love?

Epistemic certainty defenestrates compassion and throws one out of not only the mystery of life but out of relationship as well, because both compassion and relationship require wonder, openness, curiosity, and humanity. If we are to "bind up the nation's wounds" as well as heal ourselves, "compassion alone is the key," Campbell writes, and compassion alone unlocks the door to healing—and bliss.

Ego, Irony, *and the* Goddess

One of the qualities that makes myth so powerful is to be found in its exploration of reality, both material and immaterial, through the use of metaphoric irony. Ironic metaphor is effective because it intensifies and subverts reality through resemblance, and sharpens the perception, comprehension, and significance of the events and experiences that constitute the human condition. It results in "a sense of reality keen enough to be in excess of the normal sense of reality [and] creates a reality of its own" (Wallace Stevens, *The Necessary Angel: Essays on Reality and Imagination*).

As for the ego, its relationship to reality is tenuous. The ego seeks to find itself reflected everywhere and insists that the reflected ego is itself reality. Additionally, it's problematic that the ego usually oscillates between fear and desire, and "reality" is perceived largely within that dialectic:

> The fear of death is the fear of death to your ego, and the desire that the ego should enjoy the goods that it is interested in—these are what keep you from realizing your immortality. Fear and desire are the clashing rocks that exclude us from the intuition of our own immortal character (Joseph Campbell, *Goddesses: Mysteries of the Feminine Divine*).

The ego's insistence that its own reflection is really reality is made more complicated by the fact that we simply do not know ourselves. But ignorance of oneself is a hard thought for the ego to bear, and subsequently the ego finds it too painful to live in the gap between what it wants reality to be and what reality is. Metaphor and irony compellingly explore that gap, which, when we more closely examine it, reveals itself to be a seam or a scar that knits together that which we think we know and what we don't (or can't) know. Living in and exploring the gap necessarily diminishes and distresses the ego because it is forced to become a witness to, rather than the creator of, phenomena. Because the ego expects to find its own reflection everywhere, the failure to decenter the ego results in reducing myth to an amusement, an inconsequential role-playing diversion whose object is merely to match qualities to archetypes while entirely ignoring the reality, and especially the force of the archetypal.

So how does one "get around" the ego? How can the ego be decentered? One way, and I think it's an exceptionally effective way, is to cultivate a sense of the ironic. Irony is the pin that pops the ego's inflation, calms its desires and fears, and allows one to live more enthusiastically, more gallantly, more genuinely amidst what Wordsworth called "the still, sad, music of life." Soren Kierkegaard put it this way:

> Irony is a disciplinarian feared only by those who do not know it, but cherished by those who do. He who does not understand irony and has no ear for its whispering lacks *eo ipso* what might be called the absolute beginning of the personal life. He lacks what at moments is indispensable for the personal life, lacks both the regeneration and rejuvenation, the cleaning baptism of irony that redeems the soul from having its life in finitude though living boldly and energetically in finitude (*The Concept of Irony: Kierkegaard's Writings, Volume 2*).

Irony turns things inside out and upside down; it upends and reverses things. Irony deconstructs and overthrows; it draws attention to the discrepancy between literal meaning and essential meaning. Myth, properly read, is always ironic. While the ego fears its decentering as a literal death, from the perspective of metaphysical irony, the death of the ego heralds the experience of the transcendent.

In many traditions the great Goddesses are often found in relationship to darkness and the depths, the telesterions of life where one is exposed to fear and sorrows, even to tragedy. In those dark manifestations, She is the Initiatrix who cleanses the doors of perception, which open to the transformation of consciousness and the transcendent. But the benefit of those experiences—experiences that "normal," daylight consciousness always fails to understand and would rather pathologize—is that the ego cannot extend itself fully into these dark depths. So it is there, in darkness and uncertainty, disabused of the comfort of the ego's pleasing illusions, that we are confronted with who and what we really are. She, with her dark materials, pushes us along toward individuation and wholeness. "The rapture of the tragedy is the rapture of seeing the form broken for a flowing through of the radiance of the transcendent light" (Joseph Campbell, *Goddesses: Mysteries of the Feminine Divine*).

Irony is the indispensable attitude for engaging the goddess in her depths and darkness, darkness that places the radiance of transcendence in bold relief. Irony is life's language; it grants one multiple points of view. It lets one see oneself seeing oneself, and, mercifully, irony saves us from sarcasm, cynicism, and desuetude, the demoralized manifestations of broken hearts.

Perhaps you've looked around and noticed how unforgiving and thoughtless culture is becoming; aesthetic sensibilities wane as we flirt with the neobrutalism that encroaches upon so many aspects of contemporary life. It is irony that frees us from the conventional constraining literalism of existence. Through irony we might see more deeply into the metaphor that is life, and in so seeing grow wiser, more joyful, humbler, and indeed more compassionate.

MYTH: THE GRAMMAR *of* CREATIVITY

Many of my friends and acquaintances, particularly those who are writers and artists, say that *The Masks of God, Volume 4: Creative Mythology* is their favorite Joseph Campbell work. In traditional mythology, Campbell says, individuals are supposed to experience

> certain insights, sentiments, and commitments. In what I am calling "creative" mythology, on the other hand, this order is reversed: the individual has had an experience of his own—of order, horror, beauty, or even mere exhilaration—which he seeks to communicate through signs; and if his realization has been of a certain depth and import, his communication will have the value and force of living myth.[...] Mythological symbols touch and exhilarate centers of life beyond the reach of vocabularies of reason and coercion (from *Creative Mythology*).

I prefer to understand myth more as a mode of thought or a condition of imagining rather than an explicit narrative containing a traditional, historical, or even metaphysical body of knowledge. As Professor Campbell suggests in the quote above, myth is something more than a vocabulary, and from the perspective of myth as a mode of thought, I understand myth to be something like the grammar of creativity, or the grammar of imagination.

Grammar is not merely about the proper use of language, tense, or punctuation; grammar analyzes narrative structures and makes one be aware of the constraints or limitations of various communications, conventions, and even forms of art. The English word *grammar* is related to the Greek phrase *grammatikè téchnē*, which means the "art of letters," and David Crystal believes that "grammar is the structural foundation of our ability to express ourselves." Expressing our own experiences, especially the puzzling, ineffable, sublime experiences, are, as Campbell notes, communications that have the value and force of living myth.

Myth was rediscovered during the Enlightenment because, as a mode of thinking, it was believed to be a key to comprehending history, philosophy, religion, art, linguistics, and creativity itself. Considering myth to be a master discipline that stimulates a mode of thinking frees it from the viselike grip of divine revelation and institutional oversight and returns ownership of myth to individual human beings. It freed the mythic imagination to be employed in a wide-ranging, nonlinear, exploratory search for the significance of a human life lived in a fundamentally enigmatic world. Thinking mythically frees myth from the world of supernatural intervention and rightfully reclaims for human beings an experience of the sublime that is exclusively linked to human passions, changes of fortune, joys and depressions, pathos and elation.

Myth is also a mode of thinking that reliably rewards a reader's attention with an experience of delight, even though the myth itself may address horrific themes or events. John Dryden has noted this function at work in the mythopoetic genre, not to mention all manner of poets, writers, painters, and classically educated people. The poet is, as the word *poiēsis* suggests, a maker and a creator, one whose aim is to make something beautiful, something that stirs us, not by representing things exactly as they are but by heightening their intensity and deepening their depths, qualities which Dryden termed "lively" and "just" in his "Essay of Dramatic Poesy." Mythopoesis is a uniquely human endeavor and delighting in it allows one to, if not exactly remake the world, at least remake our own reality here and now. For there is no fear in delight, no pain, no thought; delight is pure experience and is in itself transcendent.

Poïēsis and drama also instruct, writes Dryden, but the function of instruction is secondary in his mind; in his thinking, primacy of place is given to the function of delight. Delight is created by the contemplation of beauty, and the job of the creative person is to create a form of communication, a grammar, that highlights beauty and contributes to the pleasures of the soul. The condition of delight taken in every aspect of life, even in its "order, horror, beauty, or even mere exhilaration" as Campbell noted above, allows one to accept one's all-too-human existence without the slavish and frequently unbecoming obsession with transcendence, which, when it is the only goal of a spiritual practice, is simply an attempt at escaping the human condition.

By following your bliss, Campbell doesn't mean escaping from life or one's corporeality. Rather, I understand him to mean that bliss is found in the realization that life is often accompanied by inescapable constraints of one kind or another, but in spite of that, we need not respond to any controlling authority other than a deeply felt, inner sense of a central organizing principle—"the dynamism of being," as Campbell called it— an inner depth that continually unfolds in proportion to how intensely we approach our own self-becoming. Jung called it individuation, Nietzsche called it *Amor Fati*, and Keats put it this way in "Sleep and Poetry":

though no great minist'ring reason sorts
Out the dark mysteries of human souls
To clear conceiving: yet there ever rolls
A vast idea before me, and I glean
Therefrom my liberty

Much like language itself, the language and grammar of myth are capable of absorbing and disturbing us in secret ways, and often, to our own excitement or frustration and bewilderment, expose us to a vast idea. It's true, isn't it, that the mythic narratives themselves are not as important as the dialogues we have about myth and meaning? Isn't that the great inheritance, the great gift of myth: they draw us into the existentially puzzling phenomena we'd rather not have to give too much thought to, phenomena such as the mystery of existence, the constant struggle between free will and fate, and all the conditions of life that remain stubbornly resistant to the intellect and reason?

Myths expose us to the forces and effects of a complex, often overwhelming world upon a limited human being, but they also suggest to us that if we can only begin to think and imagine more mythically, we may not only feel, but actually be, less constrained by the complexities and limitations of human life. That is where liberty truly abides. Imagined and thought of this way, myth offers a closer and truer relationship with life. It certainly doesn't remove or solve the problems of living, but it illuminates the project of living from a multitude of different perspectives, and that is, if nothing else, something significant and well worth having.

Dear *and* Gorgeous Nonsense: The Poetic Impulse *in* Myth

There is something about existence that has been puzzling to human beings since the beginning of our species: a nagging intuition, an impression—an apprehension, really—that there is much more to life, that something is going on behind the material experience of the world as we understand it. Life is, in its cool, remote objectivity, inherently baffling and stubbornly impenetrable. This quality of inscrutability may certainly inspire delight, curiosity, adventurousness, and investigation, but the same impenetrability that inspires such optimism may awaken, in equal amounts, dread and fear.

Schopenhauer and Nietzsche (and more recently Emil Cioran and Eugene Thacker) persistently questioned the perspective of optimism. To dismiss these philosophers as merely nihilistic is to misunderstand their deep connection to life, their magnificent empathy for vulnerability, which gives rise to apprehensions about the "normal" sunny orientation to life and questions conventional thoughts regarding how we "should" feel and think about it. They have created philosophies that, in important ways, seem to stand against philosophy itself, against epistemological certainty and unfailing optimism. Their philosophies work to disconcert and disquiet the anthropocentrism that has characterized humanity's view of the world, a view which seems to continually frustrate human beings and their attempts to live in harmony with the conditions of life. These conditions, by the way, were established long, long before human beings were a presence in the world to bear witness to them, and are so dark that they must be seen through a poetic lens lest one lapse into complete despair.

Cioran used to refer to himself as *un homme de fragment,* a fragmented man. Life is often a fragmenting force, and one of the principal means of our fragmentation is finding oneself torn between the beguiling charms of Plato's metaphysical ideal forms, which exist in an unreachable abstract state, and the immediate experience of mind, matter, and consciousness, which we generally refer to as material and therefore "real." So what does one make of this fragmentation, of having one's mind simultaneously in the real while longing for the ideal? How does one refrain from waging war on life and manage to, as Nietzsche put it, affirm not only oneself but all existence?

The natural impulse is to devote oneself to one and dismiss the other categorically, thereby avoiding the dissonance of having to entertain two competing psychic realities. Once we've dispelled one of these possibilities, we set about trying to perfect the real or, conversely, intensify our investment in, and longing for, the ideal. In *The Mythic Dimension: Selected Essays 1959–1987,* Joseph Campbell insists that the function of art is not "annihilation [of one condition or the other], but celebration." We are better served by thinking yes/and rather than either/or, by valorizing the type of thinking reflected in "the true poetry of the poet" rather than "the poetry overdone of the prophet, and the poetry done to death of the priest."

The prophets and the priests tend toward literal, concrete interpretations of mythopoesis, and they tend to use substantive language when speaking or writing about God. From that frequent and customary usage, they assume that every substantive idea or expression has an actual, substantial *something* behind it. As a result of this overdetermined presumption, they degrade a poetic notion to prosaic pronouncements and come to understand God as an actual thing or being instead of a metaphor for some ineffable truth. The word *god* loses its metaphorical nature and is subsequently related to and relied upon as though God were a real entity. Campbell puts it this way:

> For if it is true that "God is not like anything: hence no one can understand him by means of an image," . . . then it must be conceded, as a basic principle of our natural history of the gods and heroes, that whenever a myth has been taken literally its sense has been perverted; but also, reciprocally, that whenever it has been dismissed as a mere priestly fraud or a sign of inferior intelligence, truth has slipped out the other door.

Mythopoesis, true poetry, is the foundation of religious thought; regrettably, the poetry of religion is, as Campbell noted, "done to death" by the clergy and rendered unimaginatively into uninspired prose and concretized dogma. The poetic impulse inspires what William James described as the potential for the "ontological wonder" and "cosmic emotion" that may be found in religion, and similarly it lives in the first function of myth, which Campbell says in *The Masks of God, Volume 4: Creative Mythology* is to "waken and maintain in the individual an experience of awe, humility, and respect, in recognition of that ultimate mystery, transcending names and forms, 'from which,' as we read in the Upaniṣads, 'words turn back.'"

Because it's constituted by metaphor, poetry allows us to

glimpse the ideal while still rooted in the real. It allows, even encourages, the double vision we need to make sense of this terrifying and fascinating mystery of existence—*mysterium tremendum et fascinans,* as Rudolph Otto put it—and see in it an attitude of play, the divine play of spirit, the play of the *élan vital,* the dynamism of life itself. Nobility of spirit, the supremely aristocratic point of view, Campbell says, is "the ability to play, whether in heaven or on earth," and always accompanying play are its daughters, laughter and delight. Play clarifies and unburdens; it lightens the load and often transforms judgment into appreciation. For example, Samuel Taylor Coleridge affectionately called Plato's philosophy "dear, gorgeous nonsense," and Lionel Trilling called *Finnegans Wake* "transcendent genial silliness" that in its way "keeps the world in its right course."

Humans come and go. Of course we are mortal, of that there can be no pretending, and as such we must perish. But play itself is immortal, and the game goes on, constantly refreshing itself with new players. One can sense how, if we stand with one foot in the real and one foot in the ideal—the posture of divine play—we may glimpse the transcendent truth. It's understandable, isn't it, that this two-footed standpoint—the double vision that mythopoesis confers—allows us to revel and play in and among both realms? The poetry of myth is such that we can embrace the immanence of the transcendent Platonic vision without sacrificing empirical reality. Such poetic play cultivates whimsy and affectionate good humor, so much so that we may say, "I love this dear, gorgeous nonsense of life!"

The Foolish Things *of the* World Confound *the* Wise

A picture is worth a thousand words, or so the old saying goes, and the images of tarot are laden with archetypal significance—so much so that those thousand words barely begin to open the symbolic, representational, elements of those images.

The image of the Fool in tarot is the first (or last) card of the tarot deck, and it bears the number zero. Zero is not a counting number, and similarly the Fool cannot be counted on to behave predictably or conventionally. From a traditional point of view, the Fool is a zero, a nobody, one to be ridiculed and degraded. The Fool is thought to be impulsive, irresponsible, unorthodox, unmannered, an empty-headed, naive simpleton who lacks good judgment. The Fool is often understood to be graceless, senseless, and ugly, sometimes even deformed. He may be represented as a dwarf, crippled, or otherwise deformed. Fools may also be incredibly pompous while simultaneously being shockingly incompetent. But there is another, deeper side to the Fool, an aspect that is the most important of this multifaceted, bewildering, disturbing, frustrating, and yet ultimately revitalizing creative archetype: the Wise Fool.

Usage of the word *fool* was quite common in 1800, but over the next two hundred years fell out of fashion. By 1980 or so, it was seldom used. Around the year 2000, usage of the word *fool* once again became more common; now, in 2023, it's used nearly as often as it was in the year 1800. Why has this word made a comeback, and why now? That's always the therapeutic question, you know: Why this symptom, and why is it expressing now? The forms always emerge before understanding, just as the disease has always progressed before symptoms emerge.

The image of the Fool, like all archetypal images, is timeless. Archetypes are not rigidly bound to any particular time, place, or situation, but they can be constellated and shaped by the energies of a given age and place. The idea of foolishness, and therefore the image of the Fool, seems to be constellated by difficult, dangerous times, eras that may be metaphorically represented by arid and distorted landscapes—Waste Land situations, one might say, in which hearts have become hardened and heads have become empty and addled. In the sociopolitical climate of the early 2000s, when the word *fool* returned to common use, fear dominated the emotional landscape of the time, of terrorism, of political opponents, of the truth, as well as a new fear much harder to understand: the fear of the mutability, the relativity, of truth.

We seem to be living at a time in which conservatism—as an idea, as a psychic perspective or a sociological reflex, as opposed to a political philosophy—is becoming more and more popular primarily because the conservative perspective, in its preference for order and rules, stability and traditional values, offers an escape from modernity and the bewildering uncertainty of postmodernism. The more rapid the pace of change in a society, and the more frangible, malleable, and unfathomable life becomes, the more appealing conservatism is.

Conservatism, with its hunger for rules and black-and-white thinking, sets the stage for the appearance of the transmogrifying, chaotic wisdom of the anarchic Fool (think of Groucho Marx movies with shipboard staterooms filled to overflowing with all sorts of people, the manic comedy of Robin Williams, or the revolutionary satire of Lenny Bruce and Mort Sahl). When societies and cultures become too proscribed, too rigid, or too rule bound, the Fool, through his militant anarchy, turns institutions and logic upside down and inside out. Jesus himself often occupied the role of the Wise Fool, and in Matthew 20:16 Jesus taught, "So the last shall be first, and the first last," demonstrating the foolish ability to invert and subvert the usual order of things, rebelling against the excesses of wealth and privilege and the exercise of grim authoritarianism. Echoing the words of Jesus, the tarot Fool may also be the first card or the last, which adds a kind of symmetry or circularity to the chaos of subversion.

Since irony is the primary constituent in the language of myth, perhaps the Fool is the personification of myth itself because irony is the language of foolishness. Irony intensifies and subverts reality just as the Fool does. Like the Fool, irony turns things inside out and upside down. It deconstructs and overthrows. It draws attention to the discrepancy between literal and essential meaning, all the while allowing the Fool to go about his business serenely untroubled, almost as if he's above it all, like Paul McCartney's "Fool on the Hill" watching the world spinning 'round.

The Fool sitting on the hill isn't really "above it all." He's a metaphor for the clarity of perspective, the sense of seeing a big picture while at the same time being deeply engaged in life, which reveals the interdependence of everything, that all existence is harmonious and in accord even when it appears to be a cruel, chaotic mess. It's the perspective of the deepest Self, a way of honoring one's own passions while simultaneously recognizing the limitations of being human, of following one's own heart and utilizing the wisdom of one's own mind.

Merriment and sadness are always intertwined, and an undercurrent of melancholy flows through the fool. In the second half of Shakespeare's career, the fools he created became more worldly wise, more world-weary, and consequently more compassionate. Being full of wordplay, puns, and silly jokes, the Gravedigger in Hamlet is one example of a fool. But the Gravedigger's humor conveys a deep wisdom that accepts the course and nature of life on life's own terms. He unearths a skull and tells Hamlet it was once Yorick, his father's (King Hamlet) Fool. Taken aback, Hamlet says:

> Alas, poor Yorick! I knew him, Horatio—a fellow of infinite jest, of most excellent fancy. He hath bore me on his back a thousand times. . . . Here hung those lips that I have kissed I know not how oft. Where be your gibes now? your gambols? your songs? your flashes of merriment that were wont to set the table on a roar?

He hath bore me on his back a thousand times…Here hung those lips that I have kissed I know not how oft. Hearing or reading these lines always makes me think that Yorick, the jester, the fool, must have been the main source of whatever love young Hamlet received. It was Yorick that played with the child, not his father. It was Yorick, not his vain, self-interested mother, whom he showered with kisses.

From the grave, the fool still teaches Hamlet the simple truth about living: what survives of us is love. And if we are to become fully-fledged, functional adults, the love we must pursue is not that of a parent nor that of a lover, but rather a love of the conditions of life itself. These conditions of life are not congenial to human understanding or comfort, and rather than rage against this reality, we must learn to accept, even love, the conditions of life if we are to love others, the world, and ourselves while taking a stand against hopelessness and the death of the spirit. If we can achieve this, we discover that love really is all around us—even, perhaps especially, in the company of fools.

Heroism

The following essays explore the archetypal idea of the hero from various perspectives, some of which are unconventional and perhaps not as heroic as heroism is commonly understood to be.

THE HERO *of* YESTERDAY
BECOMES *the* TYRANT *of* TOMORROW

Did you know that Joseph Campbell's perennially popular 1949 book *The Hero with a Thousand Faces* appears at number twenty-eight on *Time* magazine's list of the one hundred all-time best nonfiction books? Heroism is perennially popular in film and politics, where it has never really gone out of fashion, but heroes are particularly important to childhood. The Child Hero is certainly an archetype familiar to Jungians, but even beyond that, most of us can see how childhood itself requires acts of courage that are, from the child's perspective, heroic: wobbling, wallowing, veering up the sidewalk on your bike for the first time is, for a child, a heroic act. But to think that way about heroism, we must decenter the hero and some of the traditional assumptions about it in order to reveal how the archetype may be expressing itself in contemporary life.

Childhood is a time of uncomplicated heroes. When I recall my early childhood, I remember enthusiastically awaiting the next grainy, black-and-white rerun of *Adventures of Superman*, which I watched with a bath towel tied around my neck as a cape, or the *Lone Ranger* TV series, a dime-store mask secured by a rubber band to my face and plastic six-gun at my side. My childhood heroes had no nuance and certainly no trace of corruption or impropriety. Villains were always apprehended by the hero without deadly force or personal animus. The mid-twentieth-century hero was crafted to unambiguously personify the best of humanity, but to disillusioned modern eyes such a hero is an absurd, one-dimensional anachronism.

Heroism as a concept continues to evolve as societies and cultures evolve. For example, in the first decade of the twenty-first century, one begins to see the rise of the antihero reflected in television shows like *The Sopranos, Mad Men,* and *Breaking Bad.* Finding ourselves rooting for these deeply flawed, often ignoble and selfish, even psychopathic characters may give one pause, and compel a closer look at one's own shadowy inner world, replete with its sordid desires, nefarious characters, and unscrupulous striving for power. This is the shadow of the hero archetype, and heroism's shadow is essential; it completes the hero archetype. It's the shadow cast by the sun, the far side of the moon, the unknown. The Shadow is illusory, and a powerful, chthonic psychic presence. Jung noted that the shadow is irrational, instinctual, and prone to projections and delusions, exactly like the antiheroes possessed by it.

The shadow of heroism is emerging more and more in contemporary life, and the archetype is acquiring a darker, psychologically defensive quality, becoming, essentially, an unexamined caricature, perhaps even a banality, used to avoid wrestling with complex contemporary cultural phenomena, particularly warfare, racism, and other forms of violence. With the ascendency of shadow heroism, one needn't commit heroic acts to be heroic. When one has the unmitigated bad luck of being in the wrong place at the wrong time, and is ground up by the gears of the machinery of life while simply going about living, one's daily routine is enough to qualify as heroism.

Another prevalent quality of the antihero may be found in the tendency of onlookers to misidentify outrageous, reckless, greedy, narcissistic behavior as heroic. Indeed, if there is anything close to courage that may be found in such behaviors, it is simply the sheer audacity used to nullify social contracts and conventions while callously dismissing any concern for the well-being of society. But it isn't hard to understand why such behavior seductively appeals to individuals who feel they have been cheated by life or prevented from finding success because of the interventions of conspiratorial, hegemonic forces. These characteristics of shadow heroism possess a viral character and root themselves in contemporary life to such a degree that the beau ideal of heroism—selflessness, humility, courage, and principled ethical conduct—have become recherché and have little left in common with contemporary ideas of heroism.

The childhood fascination with heroes is undoubtedly rooted in the childhood experience of sweeping powerlessness and vexing dependence, experiences that generally evoke one of two fantasies: that of being rescued and saved, or, conversely, to become so skillful, smart, and physically unmatched that one dominates every moment, creating safety and protection while simultaneously freeing oneself to live a life uncomplicated by limits. But what happens if, for some reason, we are unable to free ourselves from the conditions of powerlessness and dependence? All that's left to us is the improbable hope that a hero will appear to save us. Eventually resignation turns to bitterness, and those humiliating feelings are compounded by even more humiliating acts of subordination to bullies, officials, institutions, and other power brokers in the often brutal sociopolitical arena. In response to this humiliation, the shadow of heroism grows deep and viciously strong.

At the same time we're crying out for traditional heroism, the shadow of heroism works against it, upending its familiar ideals and values. We've all heard comments about how

American culture loves to build up heroes, and equally loves the sport of tearing them down. We tear them down because inevitably the hero we have is not the one we want, not the perfect one we deserve. They are not the hero who reflects the fantasy of our perfect selves back to us.

When the shadow hero—the antihero—is in ascendence, one reverts to simplistic thinking, unable to see the complexities and nuances of the archetype. We're blind to the shadowy elements of heroism at work within ourselves because the shadow has malformed heroism into a dark parody of itself, insisting that overcoming our own powerlessness and need is its greatest and only justification. Far from inspiring nobility and grace, such contemporary misconceptions of heroism have set free the squalid meanness of our lives that now dominates public discourse.

"The latest incarnation of Oedipus, the continued romance of Beauty and the Beast," as Joseph Campbell so beautifully writes in *The Hero with a Thousand Faces*, may indeed be standing on the corner of Forty-Second Street and Fifth Avenue, but they no longer wait patiently for the light to change; blind and helpless, they're bolting angrily into Gotham City traffic with no other intention than to create confusion, chaos, and fear. Meanwhile, the traditional, mid-twentieth-century hero of my childhood seems nowhere to be found.

Perhaps that is all as it should be. Perhaps in the long run, we're better off without obsolete notions of heroism. Perhaps the antihero, having vanquished the conventional, classical hero, has done us the favor of forcing us to discover we don't need heroes "out there" in the world. We need to find heroism within ourselves; we need to discover that we already are the heroes we've been hoping for. That is the truly heroic turn: to attempt to consciously reach beyond the archetype in an effort to become unflinchingly empathetic, mercifully humane, and entirely *human* human beings.

THE KING WHO SAVED HIMSELF
from BEING SAVED

Heroism and adventure seem to me to be a linked pair. Reflexively, I think, we imagine adventure as a going out, an extension into the world, a leaving of the known, familiar world of domestic routines for the unknown, unpredictable, unmanageable world. This, doubtless, constitutes the often invasive bearing of the hero. But the word adventure has its roots in the Latin word *advenire*, which means to arrive, to come to, a perspective that is a bit more aligned with those who experience the arrival of the hero and the effects of the hero's exploits upon them and their communities.

One of my most beloved books is a first edition copy of *The King Who Saved Himself from Being Saved*. It's a poem written by John Ciardi that was first published in the November 14, 1964 edition of the *Saturday Review*, and published as a book in 1965, charmingly illustrated by the marvelous Edward Gorey. To get a sense of this satiric poem's chiding of heroism, let me quote from the inside of the book jacket:

> The King was dozing and thinking about his money. The Queen was pampering a cold with aspirin pies. The Princess was safely in her tower listening to a lark. The Giant, a gentle creature, being at the moment unoccupied, was sprawling beside the brook smelling a flower. The castle, the Royal Family, and the Kingdom were at peace.
>
> And then the Hero arrived, sheathed in armor, breathing flame, looking for a villain and a castle to save.

> He scared the lark. He woke the King. The Princess
> cried and the Giant hid in the closet. But the Hero went
> on stamping around and making heroic noises.

The Hero, who in this case mistook a noble calling for a mere career, makes a general nuisance of himself and creates big problems in a place where, before his arrival, there were none. "All *over* his head was his helmet," Ciardi writes, "and *in* his head was, of course, a fight." The King warned the Hero that he should move on, that he doesn't want his Kingdom "saved in two," and gave him until the count of ten to leave or be subjected to the business end of a cannon the King brought forward to emphasize his seriousness. The Hero persisted, the cannoneer fired, and the King remarked, "Well, I tried to tell him. But I guess Heroes are hard to tell." Ciardi writes, "The Kingdom was saved from being saved. The Giant was saved from a fight. The King was afraid that he had behaved in ways not entirely right." Reflecting on the Hero's demise, the King went on to say, "As Heroes go he was brave enough, but I'm not sure he was bright."

Moving out of one's familiar sphere of existence and into situations and environs with which one is unfamiliar, while at the same time stubbornly clinging to familiar values, mores, and dogmatisms, almost always results in catastrophic misadventures, as Ciardi's intrepid yet fatuous Hero demonstrated.

In myths, however, the movement from the known into the unknown is what Joseph Campbell called "crossing the threshold. This is the crossing from the conscious into the unconscious world, but the unconscious world is represented in many, many, many different images, depending on the cultural surroundings of the mythos." This threshold crossing is, Campbell goes on to say in *Pathways to Bliss: Mythology and Personal Transformation*, "simply a journey beyond the pairs of opposites, where you go beyond good and evil."

We are commonly given to the understanding that space is wide and time is deep. We too often associate adventure and heroism with space—it happens here, across these territories, at those places, at that time, and so on. So where are we going when we go "beyond good and evil"? We are going, I think, to a place that feels entirely foreign to us, beyond distinctions between space and time, a place beyond individual will where conceptual faculties like logic, reason, and differentiation are rendered powerless and we, perforce, achieve awareness of the fact we are an aspect, an artifact, of the dynamism of life.

It's not simply going beyond good and evil, beyond concepts. It is nothing less than, as Fredrich Nietzsche said, a revaluation of all values. "Crossing the threshold" means the achievement of a psychophysical awareness in which one experiences a transcendent overfullness called aisthesis. I imagine that the sensation is akin to William Blake's sublime vision: "To see a World in a Grain of Sand / And a Heaven in a Wild Flower / Hold Infinity in the palm of your hand / And Eternity in an hour."

Crossing the threshold means using one's imagination as a vessel to explore the universe without *and* within. I'm reminded of the pre-Socratic philosopher Parmenides, who insisted that that which is not cannot be thought about. Conversely, anything that can be thought about exists, and must exist. The ungenerous reader may call this nonsense, but I would prefer to call this an example of mythic thinking, mythopoesis even, which expands and opens the universe rather than diminishes it. Isn't the capacity to abstractly imagine a universe beyond concepts and oppositions—beyond good and evil—enough to encourage us to at least try to rethink, redefine, and reconsider what it is to be a self, what nature is, and who others are in the field of experience?

Of course, the Sufi poet Rumi got there a long time ago and, I think, got it exactly right when he said (as translated by Coleman Barks with John Moyne):

> Out beyond ideas of wrongdoing and rightdoing,
> There is a field. I'll meet you there.
> When the soul lies down in that grass,
> The world is too full to talk about.
> Ideas, language, even the phrase *each other*
> Doesn't make any sense.

Isn't the real adventure to attempt to be so present, so attuned to life, as to experience the overwhelming fullness of the world, the self, the world-self even, with all dogmas, illusions, and oppositions dropping away? This is the heroic adventure that is always at hand. Any time is the right time for threshold crossing if you simply say yes to the conditions of life and to imagination, and make the effort to affirm things just as they are in each of the moments you happen to occupy.

THE BOUNDARY-BLURRING
NATURE *of* MYTH

Anyone who has ever been in psychotherapy is likely to be familiar with the no-nonsense injunction to have clear, defined boundaries in order to prevent others from "invading" or ignoring your boundaries. The idea is, of course, that those solid, clearly defined boundaries are the key to a mentally healthy life. Indisputably, when it comes to emotional, physical, or sexual abuse, creating good boundaries are a necessary (but not solely sufficient) step in stopping abuse, as well as preventing further abuse. But I'd like to bracket serious pathological issues like abuse, set them aside for the moment, and instead explore boundaries from a less dire perspective.

Encountering boundaries is an inescapable feature of being human, and we should remember that boundaries are not simply human creations. Geologic features create boundaries; mountains, seas, and forests have all, at one time or another, been regarded as boundaries. Time, space, mind, and body are organically connected to boundaries. The very existence of nations, states, and municipalities are predicated upon boundaries. Perhaps the most interesting are the boundaries between inner and outer, and those are the boundaries I want to work with in this essay.

In her remarkable novel *The Black Prince*, Iris Murdoch wrote that "being a real person oneself is a matter of setting up limits and drawing lines and saying no. I don't want to be a nebulous bit of ectoplasm straying around in other people's lives." Like Murdoch's character, Bradley—one must appreciate the irony, yes?—we want to be able to imagine ourselves as single and singular individuals. We want to believe that if the limits are clear enough and the lines drawn are incisive and bold enough, we can prevent others, even the rest of the world, from "straying around" in our own lives. We'd like to think that boundaries are mostly unambiguous, self-evident, and inevitable. And yes, they certainly contribute order and clarity to the living of life, but we can't escape from the messiness, the straying around-ness, and the sordidness of life in order to enter into a discrete, highly structured, well-bounded life with aspirations to an undisturbed hermetic existence—nor should we want to.

I can't help but wonder if we would benefit from less reliance on boundaries and letting ourselves sink a bit more into the disarray and blurriness of life. Boundaries are ambiguous; what's inside and what's outside depend upon which side one's perception lies. It follows, then, that one culture's hero is another's terrorist, and one's treasure is another's trash. Additionally, where there are boundaries there are defenses. Where one is positioned and how well those defenses work determine how easily they can become self-imposed prisons.

For Joseph Campbell, the hero's adventure was all about moving beyond boundaries, and the primary mise-en-scène for the hero's adventure is found within one's own inner world. It seems that the inner world, particularly the unconscious, explicitly demands blurring the territory among, across, and around boundaries. This is perhaps why, in the mythless, unheroic age of contemporary life, Campbell emphasizes that the hero's journey is primarily an inner one, and the boon achieved is that of an expanded consciousness.

In his introduction to *The Hero's Journey*, Phil Cousineau wrote:

As a mythologist with a metaphysical slant on life, a doctor of things-beyond-appearances, [Campbell] dedicated his life to mapping out the experience of plumbing those depths, which is the journey of the soul itself. The cartography, as he drew it, was the geography of the inner or underworld, showing perilous territory to be traversed not by the faint, but by the stout of heart. If myths emerge, like dreams out of the psyche, he reasoned, they can also lead us back in. The way out is the way in. It is a movement beyond the known boundaries of faith and convention, the search for what matters, the path of destiny, the route of individuality, the road of original experience, a paradigm for the forging of consciousness itself: in short, the hero's journey.

William Blake also insisted that there is the known and the unknown, and in between them, there are doors. I would suggest that myths serve as the doors between the known and the unknown and blur boundaries, making them permeable. Myth is perpetually blurring boundaries, and I would argue that an important quality of myth is its ability to do just that. Myth constantly smudges the edges of ourselves and the world; it blurs boundaries between the material and the immaterial, between gods and humans, between past, present, and future, between ethics and morals, and between emotion and catastrophe. Perhaps all the blurring makes everything fit together better. Myth peregrinates through all these and more, leaving one to conclude that the body of myth is itself a unifying symbol. As C. G. Jung wrote, a unifying symbol is running its course in the unconscious of modern man. Between the opposites there arises spontaneously a symbol of unity and wholeness, no matter whether it reaches consciousness or not. Should something extraordinary or impressive then occur in the outside world, be it a human personality, a thing, or an idea, the unconscious content can project itself upon it, thereby investing the projection carrier with numinous and mythical powers ("Civilization in Transition," from *The Collected Works of C. G. Jung*).

Myth, because it exists and functions between opposites, becomes an important point of entry, not just to imagination and the unconscious but to the discovery of the capacity and potential of human beings. But mythology can assume this function only if we cease to understand myth as a relic, as a curiosity, a just-so story, a religion, or any other clearly defined, bounded concept. To the contrary, myth moves in and through and around life, disclosing that will-o'-the-wisp quality of the vital spark, the *élan vital*. Mythology is not merely a museum-like repository of normative or once-orthodox narratives. Mythology is the final destination of singular thought and experience, the sublimely confounding creations that cannot be repeated and are, in fact, diminished by attempts at replication. That's why when we read myth, it matters little from where the myths come or their historical context. We never fail to be moved by them.

WE ARE LIVED *by* POWERS
WE PRETEND *to* UNDERSTAND

We often don't seem to think about fear in relation to heroism. The heroic deed has usually been accomplished by the time we've heard or read of it, and by then we are more inclined to wonder at the gallantry, the audacity, and the bravery of the hero than whether they were afraid.

I think everyone probably has their own definition of fear, and harbors fears that are particular to themselves, especially those fears that come in the night, the children of the dark goddess Nix. Even Zeus feared Nix, and Virgil insisted she was the mother of the Furies. No wonder it so often seems that in darkness fear is aroused. Her children, Moros (doom), Thanatos (death), Oizys (anxiety), and Momus (blame) haunt us in the lonely dark. The Oneiroi open the doors of our dreams to their siblings, who bedevil us, disturb our sleep, and make us think, Hamlet says, of that other sleep, the sleep of death, which he dreads: "For in that sleep of death what dreams may come when we have shuffled off this mortal coil, must give us pause."

Everyone fears something. And everyone responds to their fears in their own ways. Fear is many things, but its essence is simply this: fear is everything in us that remains unfinished and unloved. We fear death because we feel an abundance of life in us; life is right there, unfinished, yet to be lived. We're not yet finished with our relationships to loved ones, to pets, or to the beauty we find in the world. The desire is always for more, more life, more experience, more joy, more love, more success . . . until it isn't. Until desire is sated. And we all understand that when it isn't anymore, when the desire for life is extinguished, it is relatively easy to relinquish.

True heroism is recognizing, understanding, accepting, and working to transform these fearful impulses and emotions within ourselves, to redefine our relationship to fear, to learn, somehow, to live with fear while at the same time refusing to be lived by it. Heroes do not attempt to compensate fear with ego-driven status, power, control, and making others quake in the presence of their might. He who seeks to overcome others and the external world by "treasons, stratagems, and spoils" remains a fear-haunted, self-terrorized individual who never delivers the compassionate boons of true heroism to his community, but instead dispenses only chaos, catastrophe, and wide-scale misery.

Every resistance to knowing ourselves is dangerous— explosively so. The condition of not knowing yourself, of being unconsciously or consciously self-deceptive, of avoiding the knowledge that you are not who you have always believed yourself to be, can quite literally destroy your life, as well as the lives of others. The way through fear is to allow oneself to move into it rather than trying to avoid it, undertaking the exploration of how fear lives in me, how it distorts my perceptions of myself, of others, and the world around me, to recognize how it narrows my focus only to the threatening, the harmful, or the malign. This is the way through fear: to see compassionately how fear is at work within me and then to shift to another vantage point that reduces fears, paranoia, and frenzied, panicked, acting out. Discovering value for compassion and locating compassion within ourselves are two important keys. Rilke once wrote to a young poet saying perhaps everything that frightens us is, in its deepest essence, something helpless that wants our love. Tremendous healing potential is unlocked when we begin to see that the fear we project into the world is really something unfinished, something un-nurtured and unloved in ourselves.

Understanding fear from this perspective is difficult, however, because the cultural message insists that to be heroic, one must be without fear. Heroism is synonymous with fearlessness in much of literature, particularly in the literature of the medieval romances. In Wolfram's Parzival, for instance, the narrative is that Parzival is fearless: "He weighed his javelin in his hand, saying: 'What have I heard? Oh, if only the Devil would come now, in his fearful wrath! I would take him on, for sure! My mother talks of his terrors—I believe her courage is daunted," and "God was in a sweet mood for breeding when he wrought Parzival, who feared few terrors." In fact, the only thing Parzival fears is disgrace.

The fear of shame is a common element in martial or chivalric cultures, and shame is certainly not limited to the Western World. Samurai culture, for instance, was deeply shame based, and in it, shame could only be redeemed by a form of ritual suicide, an act which I'm inclined to see as an unfortunate literalization of the death of the ego—egocide literalized becomes suicide. The attitude of fearless heroism places one in dangerous proximity to what Campbell, in *The Hero with a Thousand Faces*, referred to as "the inflated ego of the tyrant." Perhaps what saves Parzival from this ego-dominant position is his utter naivete.

But accepting fear is merely one part of the equation; there is also the business of *Amor Fati*, not just the acceptance of, or resignation to, our respective fates but the actual *love* of one's own fate. Professor Campbell writes that fear "is the emotion that arrests the mind before whatsoever is grave and constant in human suffering and unites it with the secret cause. What does that mean? That is the key to the whole thing: the secret cause" (*Thou Art That: Transforming Religious Metaphor*).

What is the "secret cause"? The secret cause is one's fate, one's destiny, of which the final expression is unavoidable death.

I think it's safe to say that if we have no fear, we must not be truly living. The challenge is to welcome fear as evidence that we are alive and living the life we are destined to live. But that is so difficult to do in practice because there is so much of the unknown in us and around us, so much of life is outside of individual control—the things the ego hates most. Living consists of being lived by powers that shape our lives, powers that we, as W. H. Auden wrote, only pretend to understand. Powers that push us up against limits, plunge us into the twists and turns of life, and conjure the unplanned, the unforeseen, and the catastrophic. But those same powers conjure the joyfully unexpected blessings too.

All these powers that work on us are the revelations of one's destiny. They all point to the secret cause, our own destiny, our own fate, and constitute the circumstances of our own individual lives. When we affirm *Amor Fati* we commit to not only accepting our lives but loving the life we have just as it is, not wanting it to be different in any way. If we can do that well enough, just that one thing, we set to work finishing all that is yet unfinished within us, and from that new perspective, we see everything as a revelation of the Divine. That is the true achievement of heroism.

WE HAPPY FEW

Generally speaking, fellowship is what we call the act of meeting, sharing, and celebrating life with others. It may even be proper to imagine it as a celebration of collectivity. In doing so, we share joys as well as burdens, offer advice, aid, or consolation. We encourage one another's intentions or goals. Perhaps more importantly, fellowship is a way we see one another, a way of creating a sense of belonging, of coming to know oneself through one's relationships to others. And what's more, the bonds of fellowship are strengthened when one's community finds itself in the midst of a crisis.

Take, for instance, Shakespeare's *King Henry V* and the moving speech the King makes before the Battle of Agincourt:

Old men forget: yet all shall be forgot,
But he'll remember with advantages
What feats he did that day: then shall our names
Familiar in his mouth as household words . . .
Be in their flowing cups freshly remember'd.
This story shall the good man teach his son;
And Crispin Crispian shall ne'er go by,
From this day to the ending of the world,
But we in it shall be remember'd;
We few, we happy few, we band of brothers;
For he to-day that sheds his blood with me
Shall be my brother; be he ne'er so vile,
This day shall gentle his condition:
And gentlemen in England now a-bed
Shall think themselves accursed they were not here,

And hold their manhoods cheap whiles any speaks
That fought with us upon Saint Crispin's day.

Shakespeare leaves no doubt that the bonds of love and brotherhood are forged in adversity, and such a love binds us in fellowship, fosters self-respect, and is made stronger still for having survived hardships.

Similarly, here's Joseph Campbell, remarking in *Myths to Live By*, on the brotherhood created by finding ourselves in extremis with others:

> And I have lately had occasion to think frequently of this word of Schopenhauer as I have watched on television newscasts those heroic helicopter rescues, under fire in Vietnam, of young men wounded in enemy territory: their fellows, forgetful of their own safety, putting their young lives in peril as though the lives to be rescued were their own. There, I would say—if we are looking truly for an example in our day—is an authentic rendition of the labor of Love.

It's important to point out that the battle one engages in order to form these bonds of fellowship needn't be waged in a war. It's enough that we support one another to accept the burdens of being human while facing the daily challenges of living, the inescapable struggle for dignity and freedom, peace and understanding. These quotidian challenges may arouse and reinforce our bonds of fellowship just as securely as any experience of warfare. The most important battle remains, in fact, the battle within ourselves to overcome the personal ego and recognize that what I traditionally identify as me—a distinct, self-directed, independent self—is a fundamental misunderstanding of existence and being.

The primary task of the hero is to overcome the personal ego, and if that can be accomplished, one quite naturally turns to the pursuit of relieving others' suffering. This may be understood, in Joseph Campbell's way of thinking, as the boon that the returning hero shares with the community. Such a boon not only relieves the suffering of others but also creates sharing, nurturing relationships—in a word, fellowship. The egoist (one could just as easily use the word *tyrant*) approaches others and the world with the question, what can you give me? The true hero approaches life armed with the question, what can I give you? In ancient Greece, the *symbolon* was understood to be the concrete token of a gift and had the function of transmitting the whole history of the giver into the recipient, which then continued to live on in the receiver. It is as if through giving, we discover the secret to eternal life!

Finally, it seems to be a basic truth that if human beings are to enjoy good physical and mental health, we need to be in the company of others, we need to feel that we belong to something larger than ourselves. Simply stated, we need fellowship. As I mentioned at the beginning of this essay, it is so important to find places where we may be seen—not seen through, which only elicits shame, or seen with envy or admiration, which generally leads to narcissism, but rather seen into, which is a genuinely soulful, heartful experience for both the seer and the seen. Yet no seeing, however deep, can reveal the scope or reality of the entire individual all at once. But we can see the fragments, the twinklings, the essences, or the dynamics of the real at

work in a life, and over time, through the remarkable recom-
binatory nature of memory, we fashion a more and more complete picture of a person, whom we eventually come to see and
know as a whole being. To remain unseen is a terrible wound
to the psyche, and may even be a factor in some severe mental
disorders. Campbell discusses how madness can share in the
images of myth:

> My own had been a work based on a comparative
> study of the mythologies of mankind, with only here
> and there passing references to the phenomenology of
> dream, hysteria, mystic visions, and the like. Mainly,
> it was an organization of themes and motifs common
> to all mythologies; and I had had no idea, in bring-
> ing these together, of the extent to which they would
> correspond to the fantasies of madness. According
> to my thinking, they were the universal, archetypal,
> psychologically based symbolic themes and motifs of
> all traditional mythologies; and now from this paper
> of Dr. Perry I was learning that the same symbolic
> figures arise spontaneously from the broken-off, tor-
> tured state of mind of modern individuals suffering
> from a complete schizophrenic breakdown: *the condi-
> tion of one who has lost touch with the life and thought
> of his community and is compulsively fantasizing out of
> his own completely cut-off base* (emphasis is mine).

For better or for worse, the multiformity of life in our respective communities inevitably informs and shapes our thoughts
and actions. Ideally, the fellowship we keep helps us find and

understand ourselves more deeply and extends the boundaries of our concerns beyond our own immediate interests to those of our fellows, and even to the world itself. Anaïs Nin wrote, "Each friend represents a world in us, a world possibly not born until they arrive, and it is only by this meeting that a new world is born." We must be conscious and intentional in seeking fellowship because those affiliations will determine what kind of worlds will be born in and from us, and give form to our own becoming.

The Illusions *of* Failure

Failure is, I think, more inextricably linked to heroism than success is. Failure tends to stick with us longer, while success is more chimerical, and it passes relatively quickly when we do manage to achieve it. On the road to heroism, it is a certainty that the prospective hero will fail miserably and more than once. Failure is an inevitable and, I believe, an invaluable feature of living any life, but especially the heroic life.

When I was a very young, very raw police officer, there was an older officer I looked up to. He grew up in the Bronx, did three tours of duty in Vietnam, and liked poetry, movies, and bodybuilding. We became friends, worked out together, and often found ourselves working the nightshift because he (and I, it turned out) loved the energies of darkness. We loved the unpredictability, the excitement, and the flood of adrenaline. Often, reflecting upon situations we encountered that had the potential for ending badly, he would say to me, "All the heroes are in cemeteries." I was never really sure of what exactly he meant by that. But I thought that because contemporary culture often sees death as a kind of failure, as an event that shouldn't have happened and always premature regardless of age, in the final analysis, the hero's death, while heroic, is likely to be seen as a failure rather than the simple, apt culmination of a life. I assumed he was telling me that being killed on duty (or anywhere else, really) was a failure. A mistake. An error that should have been prevented.

Over a very long time of reflection, I have come to find echoes of Sophocles in my comrade's koan-like declaration. In *Antigone,* Sophocles wrote that "one must wait until evening to see how splendid the day has been." In *Trachinae* the playwright wrote, "There is an ancient saying, famous among men, that thou shouldst not judge fully of a man's life before he dieth, whether it should be called blest or wretched." I think my partner was saying that pursuing the heroic life is likely to exhaust itself, and its logical culmination is the grave. It's destiny, and we find ourselves back with Joseph Campbell's secret cause. We human beings have a hard time judging or understanding that which is ongoing, unfolding, or underway. We are only able to begin to understand that which is finished, and the judgment of heroism may only be made when one's life has reached its end.

Perhaps that's why it's somewhat easier to assess heroism when the hero dies in midcareer. That may have something to do with why, since 1941, more than half of the Medals of Honor awarded by US presidents (in the name of Congress) have been awarded posthumously. For those who give their lives for a noble cause, some recognition of heroism is more or less assured, and these heroic dead will do nothing further to tarnish their heroism. Nothing more will be asked of them. They are eternally heroic and often eternally young, making their absence from the world all the more poignant and further burnishing the golden aura of their heroism.

But for we who yet live, life goes on. And living is no easy task, as one failure is heaped upon another. In his novel *Big Breasts and Wide Hips*, the great Chinese novelist and Nobel laureate Mo Yan reminds us that "dying's easy; it's living that's hard. The harder it gets, the stronger the will to live. And the greater the fear of death, the greater the struggle to keep on living." And, I would add, the greater the struggle to keep on living, the more bitterly we regard our failures.

But the fact of failure itself shouldn't be surprising; in fact the only surprises about failure lie in its breathtakingly innovative variations. Nevertheless, one is left with a sense that in American life failure, or the acknowledgement of it, is somehow shameful or improper. But in truth, failure is simply a negotiation with our all-too-human limitations. It is the *inaequalis magister vitae* (life's unequaled teacher), and for that reason it is, I believe, a nearly ubiquitous presence in myth. Every success is itself a form of failure, writes Joyce Carol Oates in her marvelous essay "Notes on Failure." There is always a compromise between what is desired and what is attained:

> after all, there is the example of William Faulkner who considered himself a failed poet; Henry James returning to prose fiction after the conspicuous failure of his playwriting career; Ring Lardner writing his impeccable American prose because he despaired of writing sentimental popular songs; Hans Christian Andersen perfecting his fairy tales since he was clearly a failure in other genres—poetry, playwriting, life. One has only to glance at *Chamber Music* to see why James Joyce specialized in prose.

What's more, I have to wonder if the hero isn't also unconsciously in love with failure. There is something all too final about success, something finite which is relegated to the lifelessness of past experience or history. Oates thinks that success really only lives in the past, while failure and its moments of vitalization are always with us. She may be right.

The risks one takes in facing the dangers of living, especially of following one's bliss, gives one the sensation of being jaw-droppingly alive. What else might explain the hero's penchant for that which exists in danger, mystery, and intoxicating adrenaline? Why is the hero drawn to extremes? It can only be exhilaration, the frisson of living life as though death itself was of no consequence. It's the exhilaration one feels from living as though life were a game, or as if one were an actor in a play.

Certainly, nothing about life and living is easy, not even games, if they are to continue to engage and entice us. If they were easy, we would quickly tire of them. If one understands that life is a game that demands perseverance, practice, and the ability to understand death as the apotheosis of life rather than its interruption, one may feel unfettered, much less burdened by living. The problem of life is not death but rather what we believe death to be. Culturally, we've decided that death is bad, that death is something abnormal, an anomaly of living, instead of recognizing it as an important developmental milestone that, like any other developmental marker, must be properly faced to be achieved (both C. G. Jung and Sigmund Freud noted that death is as important to human beings as birth).

Engaging life as a game captures what Joseph Campbell called the "aristocratic spirit," an attitude from which one lives life on life's own terms and engages life nobly, honestly, and courageously as play. And as the catcher Crash Davis said in the movie *Bull Durham*, there is only one way to play a game: "You be cocky and arrogant, even when you're getting beat. That's the secret. You gotta play this game with fear and arrogance."

By living this way, fear and arrogance cancel each other out, ultimately leaving one with only the serene acceptance of one's fate, the sense of *Amor Fati*, which is exactly the attitude of the hero unconsciously in love with failure. And of course, it must be love, since failure is such a large part of life, and as Joseph Campbell wrote, "Love, for [the hero] is absolute, singlefold, and for life" (*Flight of the Wild Gander: Selected Essays, 1944–1968*). Love always and in all ways is for life, for all of it, in its every manifestation. Even when it manifests in failure.

THINKING *at the* EDGES *of* JOSEPH CAMPBELL: THE FUTURE *of the* MYTHBLAST SERIES

(PUBLISHED ON OCTOBER 28, 2020, THE THIRTIETH ANNIVERSARY OF THE JOSEPH CAMPBELL FOUNDATION)

Anniversaries mark the important events of one's life; they invite reflection on the past, why it mattered, and where we've come from. Simultaneously, anniversaries stimulate thinking about the future, where we want to go, and what remains to be done. Anniversaries often find us at a boundary, a border between what we have been and what we will become. They place us at the edges of ourselves, with aspiration pressing against present limitations, and as you will see, the thirtieth anniversary of the Joseph Campbell Foundation is no exception.

In *The Death and Life of Great American Cities*, Jane Jacobs, a most remarkable woman, wrote, "Often borders are thought of as passive objects, or matter-of-factly just as edges. However, a border exerts an active influence." At the place of borders, edges, and limits, psyche exerts its influence as well, and the power of its protean creativity, its *appel à l'aventure*, awakens a desire for a more fully lived life. It is the call to adventure, and to answer it, one must be dauntless and willing to transgress apparent limits, especially the inner psychological limits defended by belief, fear, convention, or fiat—the conditions of life to which myth speaks most eloquently.

Mythology is indispensable for one engaged in the enterprise of working at the limits or the edges of oneself. Among the difficult challenges one finds at the edges of oneself is contending with psychic realities, often destabilizing personal and cosmic truths, and the disturbing intuition that, as W. H. Auden wrote, "We are lived by powers we pretend to understand: They arrange our love; it is they who direct at the end/ The enemy bullet, the sickness, or even our hand." At the edges of ourselves, thinking into myth confounds our notions of comfort, understanding, and predictability, making one confront, to gloss Gershom Scholem, the terrors from which myths are made.

In his paper "At the Edges of the Round Table: Jung, Religion, and Eranos," David Miller described his experience of attending his first conference at the Eranos Foundation in 1969. Eranos was created in 1933, and its central mission was "to provide time and space for thinking." Dr. Miller describes his experience this way:

> I first attended the Eranos Conferences in 1969. Along with Gilles Quispel and James Hillman, the speakers were Helmuth Jacobsohn, Gilbert Durand, Toshihiko Izutsu, Schmuel Sambursky, Henry Corbin, Ernst Benz, Gershom Scholem, and Adolf Portmann. The seats for the auditors at Casa Eranos were reserved, and I was assigned a seat in the fourth row. The aisle and Lago Maggiore were on my right and an elderly British woman was on my left. In the intermission of the initial lecture by Scholem, I turned to my seatmate and, in an attempt to make conversation, I asked her whether there would be a question-and-answer time following the lecture. She said to me: "You must be an American." I confessed that I was, whereupon she educated me about the spirit of Eranos. "You see," she said,

"the presenters are invited to speak at the very edge of their disciplines. If they manage this edge, they are in no better position than the audience to answer questions. It would be premature. On the other hand," she concluded decisively, "if they do not manage to speak at the edge, then they are not worth questioning in the first place!"

Edges are not ends; rather, edges are the means by which one is launched into a less defined, less mediated, less determined space, and as Dr. Miller points out, edges are rich in questions that have no immediate, authoritative answers. Initial experiences of edginess are often intoxicating, but they quickly become sobering when one discovers that the relationship between edges and meaning has been uncoupled. The loss of meaning inevitably betrays the fear that nothing remains to be discovered but emptiness. The human insistence on meaning functions as an obstacle that obliterates the edge and reveals the abyss instead.

In his 1957 Eranos lecture, Joseph Campbell sought to dislodge the idea of discovering meaning as the central pursuit of living: "What—I ask—is the meaning of a flower? And having no meaning, should the flower then not be?" A bit later Campbell concludes, "Or, to state the principle in other terms: our meaning is now the meaning that is no meaning; for no fixed term of reference can be drawn. And to support such a temporal situation, each must discover himself...without fear of the open world."

Campbell urges us to "fly to . . . that seat of experience, simultaneously without and within . . . where the meaninglessness of the sense of existence and the meaninglessness of the meanings of the world, are one" (*The Flight of the Wild Gander: Explorations in the Mythological Dimension: Selected Essays, 1944–1968*).

Unencumbered by our solipsistic search for meaning, having cast off the rusty shackles of causality, we are free (or, some have said, condemned) to live in the intense immediacy and protean liminality of edges in "the open world," to play with and create room for thought and dance joyfully in the existential vacuum.

What, then, does the MythBlast series have to do with edges, meaning, and Eranos? The MythBlast series has grown to become one of the central features of the Joseph Campbell Foundation website and its internet presence. The series has published 180 original essays to date that have highlighted and explored particular Campbell texts. They have been written in an accessible yet intelligent manner that has challenged our readers to be thoughtful and at the same time whetted appetites for reading more widely in Campbell's works.

In conversations with JCF President Bob Walter and a few other colleagues at JCF, we've come to believe that the MythBlast series may be capable of functioning something like a digital Eranos, offering a space for thinking and speculative analyses at the edges of critical Campbell texts, as well as the important intellectual, scholarly, and cultural influences that shaped him. The MythBlast series is increasingly becoming a home to creative, intellectually rigorous, and novel explorations of Campbell and mythology by authors attempting to reach beyond the safe, established, and often derivative confines of traditional scholarship.

There are still some logistical issues to work out, and I'm

unsure as to how (or if) this will be achieved, but my goal is to create an opportunity for an interdisciplinary dialogue among diverse scholars—specialists and nonspecialists alike—to consider mythology as it once was, a master discipline whose scope was not limited simply to mythology qua mythology but also to related disciplines such as psychology, philosophy, religion, and even the sciences. After all, people tend to forget that Sigmund Freud, Friedrich Nietzsche, Karl Marx, and Isaac Newton were also mythologists. Mythology changes the way we understand the world, and when we understand the world differently, we change it. So it makes sense to suggest that myth can change the world. But even if it can't, even if the vast majority of human beings choose to ignore the power of myth, it can change our lives. And if enough of us change, if enough of us explore the edges of ourselves, we necessarily change our relationship to one another and the world. Just doing that, just simply going about the familiar business of being human but doing so more consciously, with more intentionality, we change the world.

Thanks for reading.

AFTERWORD

I'd like to thank John Bucher, PhD, the executive director of the Joseph Campbell Foundation, for his support and encouragement in putting together this volume of essays in which I've explored many of the subjects related to mythology that most fascinate me.

Myth is a powerful influence in our lives. Human beings are always mythologizing, always creating stories about the world and ourselves, and the interaction between the two. And in that way, myth is always humanizing. Myth explores what it is to be human, what it is to be taken to our limits, where we encounter the immutable conditions of life that, ultimately, we must accept, as those conditions were in place long before humans arrived to experience them and are in so many ways uncongenial to the human experience.

Therefore, the metaphors of myth necessarily evoke the big existential questions: Who am I? Where do I come from? How must I live? Where do I go when I die? Myth helps us discover new perspectives, symbolic language and narratives, and powerful new images, with which we can better understand ourselves and the challenges of living more adaptively, with greater equanimity, while embracing our own passions and wisdom.

Myth functions much the same as art, in that it is not a literal or factual account of the universe or of life, but it evokes the truth of existence better than objective facts can hope to do. Myth can put us in touch with the deepest parts of ourselves and the world, and help us to integrate more of life. Life then feels less strange, less alien, and we become more aware of what C. G. Jung called our "indispensable place in the great process of being." Myths open the doors of perception to astonishment, to curiosity, to the fecundity of life with its full range of emotion and sublime experience. Thinking mythically opens one to the immediacy of the mysteries of human existence, to the possibility of experiencing life itself as art, and offers a pathway that leads to the fullest experience of being alive.

About Joseph Campbell

Joseph Campbell was an American author and teacher best known for his work in the field of comparative mythology. He was born in New York City in 1904, and in early childhood became interested in mythology. He loved to read books about American Indian cultures and frequently visited the American Museum of Natural History in New York, where he was fascinated by the museum's collection of totem poles. Campbell was educated at Columbia University, where he specialized in medieval literature and, after earning a master's degree, continued his studies at universities in Paris and Munich. While abroad he was influenced by the art of Pablo Picasso and Henri Matisse, the novels of James Joyce and Thomas Mann, and the psychological studies of Sigmund Freud and Carl Jung. These encounters led to Campbell's theory that all myths and epics are linked in the human psyche, and that they are cultural manifestations of the universal need to explain social, cosmological, and spiritual realities.

After a period in California, where he encountered John Steinbeck and the biologist Ed Ricketts, Campbell taught at the Canterbury School, and then, in 1934, joined the literature department at Sarah Lawrence College, a post he retained for many years. During the 1940s and '50s, he helped Swami Nikhilananda to translate the Upanishads and The Gospel of Sri Ramakrishna. He also edited works by the German scholar Heinrich Zimmer on Indian art, myths, and philosophy.

In 1944, with Henry Morton Robinson, Campbell published *A Skeleton Key to Finnegans Wake*. His first original work, *The Hero with a Thousand Faces*, came out in 1949 and was immediately well received; in time, it became acclaimed as a classic. In this study of the "myth of the hero," Campbell asserted that there is a single pattern of heroic journey and that all cultures share this essential pattern in their various heroic myths. In his book he also outlined the basic conditions, stages, and results of the archetypal hero's journey.

Joseph Campbell died in 1987. In 1988 a series of television interviews with Bill Moyers, The Power of Myth, introduced Campbell's views to millions of people

About *the* Joseph Campbell Foundation

The Joseph Campbell Foundation (JCF) is a not-for-profit corporation that continues the work of Joseph Campbell, exploring the fields of mythology and comparative religion. The Foundation is guided by three principal goals:

First, the Foundation preserves, protects, and perpetuates Campbell's pioneering work. This includes cataloging and archiving his works, developing new publications based on his works, directing the sale and distribution of his published works, protecting copyrights to his works, and increasing awareness of his works by making them available in digital formats on JCF's website.

Second, the Foundation furthers his pioneering work in mythology and comparative religion. This involves promoting the study of mythology and comparative religion, implementing and/or supporting diverse mythological education programs, supporting and/or sponsoring events designed to increase public awareness, donating Campbell's archived works to the New York Public Library and his personal library to OPUS Archive & Research Center, and utilizing JCF's website (www.jcf.org) as a forum for mythologically informed cross-cultural dialogue.

Third, the Foundation helps individuals enrich their lives by participating in a series of programs, including our global, Internet-based Associates program and other Joseph Campbell–related events such as webinars, podcasts, and other Campbell related publications.

For more information on Joseph Campbell and the Joseph Campbell Foundation, contact:

Joseph Campbell Foundation
www.jcf.org